HEALING AS EMPOWERMENT
Discovering grace in community

HEALING AS EMPOWERMENT

DISCOVERING GRACE IN COMMUNITY

USHA JESUDASAN

GERT RÜPPELL

World Council of Churches, Geneva

Cover design: Claude Dominique Béguin
Design and layout: Gert Rüppell
Photos: Edna Orteza, Peter Williams: PhotoOikoumene, Gert Rüppell: Ecu-Learn
ISBN 2-8254-1439-5
© WCC Publications
World Council of Churches
150 Route de Ferney, PO Box 2100
CH-1211 Geneva 2, Switzerland
Website: http://www.wcc-coe.org

Printed in France

CONTENTS

Faith healing and spiritual cures have always been part of the church's ministry. But to many, they smack of magic, of mystical claims of "impossible cures", deeply foreign to "Western" patterns of religion. Conversely, those patterns are sometimes seen as dry fruits of aging churches which have lost contact with the living source of healing power. In the midst of this tension, the world's greatest contemporary pandemic, HIV/AIDS, is changing the concept of what the healing ministry of the church can mean.

But not only HIV/AIDS, also socio-economic injustice, genocides, wars, and ecological disasters incurred by humankind, demand healing and in this context call increasingly for a healing ministry of the churches.

Yet, healing memories and wounds inflicted on people physically and mentally, or allowing environment to heal, needs a long time and more importantly, it needs people who care, a healing community. The call for healing thus becomes a call for change in our relationship as a Christian community with others, with creation.

The Conference on World Mission and Evangelism (CWME) in Athens, Greece, 2005, is engaging with the challenges this situation poses to the ministry of healing of the churches. It will gather and learn from experiences made by "main-stream" churches as much as by charismatic Christians and Pentecostal churches under the theme: "Come Holy Spirit, Heal and Reconcile. Called in Christ to be reconciling and healing communities"

With *Healing as Empowerment: Discovering grace in community*, we offer a collection of stories told by participants from Asian, African and Latin-American consultations organised by the staff responsible for Mission and Evangelism in the World Council of Churches in preparation for the Conference on World Mission and Evangelism (CWME). The importance of these consultations was that they gave space for participants to share their spiritual journey as well as their personal and communal stories of healing, reconciliation and life-changing empowerment with each other. *Healing as Empowerment* aims at making these stories, from a wide variety of cultural and social contexts, available to a broader audience of readers, for their own process in and reflection on God's healing and reconciling grace.

To you the reader, we hope that this book will open your eyes to those who suffer and are in need of healing. We hope that it will encourage you to recognise your own needs for healing and for the empowerment which lies in the interaction within your own congregation, thus becoming a healing community. The stories we present show vividly how the healing ministry is lived out in different churches and Christian groups and they remind us, authors and readers alike, of our own myriad experiences of healing.

May this publication help you to realise that the healing God gives, whether it is healing of diseases, the restoration of souls, or relationships through reconciliation, is a source of life changing empowerment.

Usha Jesudasan
Gert Rüppell

ACKNOWLEDGMENT

This book is the product of all those who have participated in meetings and consultations of the team responsible for Mission and Evangelism in the World Council of Churches, where stories of healing, reconciliation and empowerment were told and shared. In particular this relates to the United Evangelical Mission's intercontinental consultation in Accra, Ghana in 2003, the World Council's consultations on Faith, Healing and Mission, Santiago de Chile, Chile in 2003 and Healing, Reconciliation and Power, Bangalore, India in 2004. We would like to thank all those who generously and graciously shared their personal stories with us. We would also like to thank the families and communities who stand behind them, often silently giving support, comfort and hope and asking nothing in return for themselves.

Many of the stories published here are part of a larger paper, describing the situation of centres, communities and congregations involved in healing. To make the book reader-friendly some of the material has been edited and academic footnotes have been removed in most cases. If you would like to obtain a full version of the document from which the adapted stories come, this can be obtained from the team on Mission and Ecumenical Formation of the World Council of Churches. At various points the publication cites quotations by His Holiness Aram I of the Armenian Apostolic Church (Holy See of Cilicia). The full text from which these citations stem can be found under "Healing - Empowering, Transforming and Reconciling Act of God" Conference Preparatory Paper No. 12 (http://www.mission2005.org).

We would also like to gratefully acknowledge Edna Orteza, Christian Educator in the Philippines and former staff member of the WCC, who gave us pictures from her work in "healing education".

As authors and editors, writing your stories and experiences has been a very enriching and empowering experience for us. Our very sincere and deep appreciation and gratitude to all those who have contributed to this book. You have been a beacon of hope and light for us and we are sure that those who read your stories will be touched and empowered too.

Usha Jesudasan
Gert Rüppell

ISSUES IN HEALING

There are many issues that come to mind when we think of healing. We know that suffering and disease have been with us from the beginning of time and throughout history humankind has reacted to pain and suffering in the same way by asking the questions: "Why pain? Why suffering? Why me?" and seeking to find some meaning in its suffering.

When we are sick or in pain, our greatest hope is for healing. The amazing hand of God has provided many channels through which one can receive healing. When confronted by disease, most people go straight to a doctor or hospital. Some prefer alternative traditional medicines or systems that are special to their culture like acupuncture/ayurveda/yoga/reiki/shibashi etc. Others try massage or exercise, or speak with counsellors to relieve stress and pain. Many, whatever their faith traditions, put their faith in God and healing through the power of prayer.

Whatever the channel we pursue for our healing, sometimes we are cured, sometimes we are not. Even if we are not cured physically, often we are healed of the wounds we carry in our soul. Those who have not been cured of their physical diseases but whose souls have been healed say that this kind of healing is what really matters.

THE MYSTERY OF SUFFERING

To someone facing pain and suffering it feels as if they have been specially singled out and broken to pieces. But as we look around, we see that actually brokenness is the norm. It is almost a way of life for many people. We see people suddenly struck by disease, difficult situations, victims of violence, divorce, and natural calamities through no fault of their own. Sometimes pain and suffering is self-inflicted and the hurting person causes pain to others. Often, suffering seems undeserved and cruel. There is no justice to it. To those who are in pain, there are no answers that make sense. No one can make the pain go away. It just has to be endured.

The desire and need for healing is not a 21st century phenomenon. It has been with us from the beginning of humankind.

We see suffering, broken people trying to make some sense out of their shattered lives. We see them weeping, running away from their pain, questioning God, learning to face their pain and finally learning to accept and respect suffering. Then we see their lives transformed and dignified by suffering. We see their lives deepened by beauty and compassion. We see them bringing compassion, comfort and hope to others in a way that they could never have done before their suffering. We also see suffering turning people into hard, withdrawn, bitter, angry people.

When pain and suffering touch our lives we are desperate to find meaning in it. Some tell us that pain is God calling us to stop and listen. Others say that there is no meaning to it. Pain and suffering is a mystery – a mystery we cannot fathom and therefore fear. A mystery which once it touches us, can either surprise us and force us to turn our lives around and into the presence of God in an act of worship, submission and love, or lead us in the opposite direction where we lose faith and turn away from love and compassion and become hard and embittered.

PAIN AND SUFFERING CRY OUT FOR HEALING

The desire and need for healing is not a 21st century phenomenon. It has been with us from the beginning of humankind.

"How long, O Lord? Will you forget me forever?" cried the battered and bruised Psalmist of old. We too use the same words during times of great suffering and pain. We know that Jesus brought healing to many who were sick. The disciples who followed Jesus took on the mantle of healing from him and since then healing has been an important part of the mission of the church.

The crucified Christ assures us that suffering and death is not the end. That no matter what we have to face in the form of sickness, disease and earthly trials, we will not be destroyed for ever.

We are hard pressed on every side but not crushed; perplexed, but not in despair; persecuted but not abandoned, struck down, but not destroyed. (2 Cor. 4:8)

WHO ARE WE ?

In the context of the healing ministry, we need to recognise whether we are the wounded in need of healing, or whether our wounds have been healed and thus we are in a position to reach out and be a source of healing for someone in pain.

There is no one who is not in need of healing. All of us have experienced brokenness in some form, be it sickness, or breakdown in family relations, betrayal, pain caused through broken relationships. Sometimes we are the ones who have been hurt; at other times we have caused hurt to others.

The heaviness of pain and suffering makes it impossible for life to go on normally. It fills our whole being. It takes over every aspect of our lives. It is hard to see or focus on anything but the pain. Often, pain takes away our sense of being. It brings feelings of emptiness, loneliness, neglect and alienation - all of which dehumanize us. All of us have experienced this at some time and understand well what the author of this poem is saying.

Sometimes I cry out in pain,
I'm hurt, I grieve, I'm dying.
I need someone to take away my pain.
I need someone to hold my hand
And take me through the darkness.
Can no one hear me?
Can no one heal me?
I feel like a worm, twisting and turning
To avoid the sharp blades through which I must pass.
But there are times when despite my pain
I know that I am not the lowly worm,
I am in fact fearfully and wonderfully made.
I am made in the image of God,
To be His beloved.
I am strong like the olive tree in the house of God.
There was once one who also bore much pain.
And cried out in his agony for respite.
He showed us how to bear our pain
and reach out to others who were suffering too.
Knowing this, I have the strength to reach out to you.
The one who in spite of my brokenness
Can see the tears in your eyes.
I am the one who will hold your hand,
the one who will take you through the darkness of
your night,
the one who will hear your cry of pain.

© Gert Rüppel: Ecu-Learn

THERE IS NO ONE WHO CANNOT BE PART OF THE HEALING CIRCLE

Do you remember the story of the woman Jesus met at the well? A woman who had had several husbands, who was an outcast burdened by her past. Jesus, when he met her, looked into her heart and understood her shame, the isolation she felt and the pain it brought her. She knew that he was the Christ, and accepted the healing he offered her. Excited, and filled with the joy of healing and the hope of new life, she ran back to her village and brought others who were also burdened and broken, so that they too could see the Christ and receive healing.

The healing that Jesus brought her was a liberating force. "I am a woman with a painful past, yet, now I am healed of those memories and the pain they brought me. I now have the power to understand others who bear such pain. I can reach out to them and help them heal too." The woman at the well, the woman caught in adultery, the paralysed man, Zachaeus, Matthew, the tax collector and the blind man whom Jesus healed, were all very ordinary people. And yet, they were all part of the healing ministry of Jesus.

As Christians, we too, whoever we are, are called to be part of Christ's ministry of healing to the world. Healing points to all the different ways through which people are liberated and reconciled in our world, and how the world itself is also being healed and reconciled.

Healing is the restoration of the brokenness of life and the recovery of life all around us.

WHO ARE WE - WHO ARE CALLED?

We are the ones who leave early in the morning
to work all day.
We are the ones who feed our children,
who nurse the sick
who cook and clean for other people,
who repair and serve,
who stand with pointed guns at border towns,
who count the money
who lay down the law.
We are the church at the corner with the tall steeple,
the village church with a thatch roof.
The church that is overflowing
and the one that is almost empty.
We are the hurt ones who carry the pain
of betrayals at home and at work,
of divorce,
of violence,
of greed.
Do we need healing?
Of course we do, for our pain is raw and deep
from rape and murder,
violence and abuse,
neglect and abandonment,
poverty and war,
unemployment and disease.

We hold out our hand,
someone reaches out,
the balm on our wounds
soothes and heals.
Together we now reach out
to hands that are stretched out to us,
to bodies that are crippled with pain,
to communities that are torn apart.
We bring the balm of healing,
of forgiveness,
of reconciliation.
We are called to the healing ministry
to do small acts of service and love,
which will help heal and transform
the wounded world

CALLED TO BE WOUNDED HEALERS

All of us are wounded in some way. Usually we are embarassed by our wounds and like to hide them away. The gospel stories encourage us not to hide our wounds, but to allow them to help us serve others who are also wounded.

"We understand wholeness, not as a static balance of harmony, but a building and living in community with God, with people and with creation. Individualism and injustice are frequent barriers to community-building and therefore to health. The members of the early church chose to share their possessions and enter into mutual dependency and accountability.

A healing community is not a world without problems and suffering, but rather a striving together to live in God's kingdom. Jesus joined the marginalized, the downtrodden and the imperfect. Through his willingness to identify,

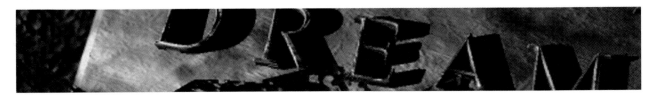

suffer and empty himself, he gave hope, restored dignity and created community. He led the marginalized back to their own communities, and enabled them to restore their relationships.

A true community is not closed. It cuts across class, status and power structures. Its members must risk moving out to identify with people who are on its fringes, inviting the marginalized and oppressed in, enabling them to join their communities with restored relationships. It is a life-giving organism with movement in and out, steadily giving rise to new organisms of healing and fellowship.

Participating in such a fellowship may be costly. It can involve leaving "father" or "mother". It is an ongoing process of self-emptying and an openness to sharing and receiving. There is not true community without giving up something. There is no coming together in community without tears. As part of a creation which is moaning in pain and longing for its liberation, the Christian community can be a sign of hope, an expression of the kingdom of God. We are called to be "wounded healers." (Health, Healing, Wholeness, 1990) A good example of "wounded healers" in today's society

are members of Alcoholics Anonymous. They have the courage to tell their stories, to acknowledge their wounds and failures. They let the others know that "I am not any better than you." But they also tell gratefully the story of how they found strength through help from other alcoholics. They share the profound conviction that, "If I, with all my scars, could do it, surely you can, too!"

This model is not restricted to the healing of alcoholics: its powerful dynamics are transplanted into other fields as well. My own experience of being completely laryngectomized gives me a unique opportunity to help others who are already or may soon be in the same situation. Those especially who, like myself, experience drawbacks should be encouraged not to give up, but to muster their inner resources of strength to discover a deeper meaning for their re-adjustment. It is well-known that the best helpers of cancer patients can be others who have experienced the same problems and are still faced with them. It is to be hoped that both doctors and the church will learn to mobilize these "wounded healers".

(Bernhard Hearing "Healing & Revealing – European WCC Consultation)

13

For you to reflect

⇨ *Have you ever felt like the Psalmist crying out: "How long, O Lord?"*

⇨ *What kind of suffering have you experienced? Did your pain cause you to withdraw and become hard and angry or did it soften you and make you reach out to others?*

For you to discuss

⇨ *What comes to mind as you read the poem "Who are we?"*

⇨ *There is no one who has not experienced pain. There is no one who has not been healed in some way. As a community or group, between you you have a wealth of experience. As an individual and as a community you are "wounded healers". Knowing this, in what ways can you reach out to those around you who suffer in some way?*

For you to meditate

Almighty God,

Creator and sustainer

Of all that is truly good,

destroyer of all evil:

I bring myself,

The family of humankind

And this physical world

In front of you,

And experience your healing power of love

You the perfect One,

are spreading rays of harmony, peace and happiness

Over me and all the world.

Your healing vision

Falls on us all

Inspiring us to seek

Only peace and unity

And an end to all suffering

(Anonymous)

HEALING
AS A NEED

We were created to be whole, and in harmony with all of Creation. Yet, as we look around us, we see that brokenness is the norm. Any kind of fragmentation or brokenness in our lives results in disharmony in our soul. Thus, all of us have a deep need for healing planted within us.

In our world today there is much that breaks up the harmony of Creation and causes pain and suffering. War, poverty, disease, the abuse of women and children, the exploitation of migrant people and the marginalized, the effects of greed and lust for power, sex and unbridled consumerism are just some of them.

To those who face the pain of these destructive forces, healing is a desperate need. Some search for it through drugs, alcohol, sex, work or accumulating wealth and possessions. But ultimately there comes the realisation that none of these bring the healing they badly desire.... the need persists and gnaws away at their souls.

THE SEARCH FOR WHOLENESS

In our quest for the meaning of health, healing and wholeness, we hear the groaning of creation in various parts of the world. We also note the "birth" and "growing pains" of programmes that demonstrate what it means to be healing communities. Health, healing and wholeness are inextricably linked to the socio-economic, cultural, spiritual and political realities of society.

There are special problems unique to countries which are moving toward industrialization and to those with full industrialization. Yet they are interdependent. Violation and destruction of the environment in one part of the world impacts the ozone layer which covers all our world. Pressure to meet the demands for goods of the northern hemisphere lure countries of the South to expand cash crops and production of goods for export which can reduce their production of essential food and basic commodities at home.

Diakonia is the healing action of the eucharistic community.
The therapy that the church experiences and proclaims in the eucharist must result in a therapy for the whole world.
(HH Aram I)

Political and economic policies of rich countries disrupt the daily lives of people elsewhere. Direct or indirect supply of weapons and other means of warfare affect the health of many. The demand for payment of international debts cripples the economies of debtor nations. The tragedy is often worse because the projects for which the debt was created did little to enhance the lives of the people of that country. The creditor nations are harmed as well, since the debtor nations are left without resources to buy their products.

All of these issues negatively impact health and wholeness. Christians recognize that the actions of governments and transnational corporations, in a quest for power, market control and wealth, interfere with the Christian quest for health, healing and wholeness.

In many countries, repressive governments are installed by those who have interests to protect.

The number of wars has increased and become a viable form of solving territorial and resource problems leaving huge numbers of people with no other choice but to escape the conflict area and become refugees ending up in camps, with little hope for return and with hardly any access to health services.

Sham elections sometimes give the appearance of democracy, but ultimately important decisions are made by those with power and affluence. Their power ensures their repeated re-election. When people become aware of injustices, their protests are ignored or met with violence. The solution may require Christians to be involved in the realm of politics.

In all this it is the poor who are most susceptible to the preventable communicable diseases, many of which occur in the context of lack of food, clean water, migration. In many cases they have multiple diseases so that even if one disease is cured, another illness may finally claim the person's life. Children are the most vulnerable group. If malnutrition in early life does not kill them, it will retard their physical and mental growth and development.

THE LONGING FOR HEALING TODAY

A primary focus of religious expectations in the 21st century is the multidimensional longing for

© Gert Rüppel: Ecu-Learn

healing of body and soul, of spirit and mind, of personal and social relations, of political and ecological dimensions in this broken world. Deteriorating health standards, the HIV/AIDS pandemic and the growing vulnerability of the human body underline the urgency of addressing the missionary challenge of global longing for healing. The number of persons suffering from depression, from mental disturbances, from loneliness and burn-out syndromes is dramatically on the increase as people cannot cope any more with the general acceleration of constant changes, increasing demands and growing insecurity in their personal life situations. Those churches which address this longing for healing in their religious life are growing worldwide. The rediscovery, the encouragement and deliberate training of the healing gifts or healing charismata within the Christian community is therefore of crucial importance for the future of Christianity everywhere, including in the West.

(D. Werner, Germany, full paper see Appendix)

We are all familiar with the story of Jesus healing the woman who had been hemorrhaging for twelve years. It was a time when women with such a disease felt cursed, were cast aside and had no hope of being normal. The woman, desperate in her need for healing just reached out and touched the hem of Jesus' cloak and was healed immediately.

Twenty one centuries later, the need for healing for many women with the same sickness still persists. But sadly, Jesus no longer walks our roads. So who will reach out and heal in His name?

HEALING ANCIENT AND MODERN

Once, I was in India with the Council of World Mission for a workshop. At the workshop there was a woman who for some reason hardly ever came to the meeting. A lot of money had been spent to bring her to the workshop and she was expected to take the message of the programme back to the people in her country. Knowing this, she still preferred to sleep in her room. As conference organizers we were really concerned. I was the keynote speaker and after sharing the story of Jesus healing the bleeding woman I challenged the listeners to take their places in the story. That evening, the woman came to talk to me. She told me that she had been bleeding for twenty years and that she was badly anaemic and could not concentrate on anything. She told me she had a huge growth in her womb, but that because she comes from a small and poor island where they have no hospital to do such an operation, she needed to be sent to Australia for it. But to be sent, the government had to approve. The government, in this case, was very poor and already owed the Australian hospitals a lot of money and they only sent important people. "I do not know what to do", she said.

> *Healing is the restoration of the brokenness of life. Healing is essentially recreation. It is recovery and rediscovery of life's wholeness, coherence and unity. (HH Aram I)*

It was a very startling moment for me. I had moved from talking theoretically and philosophically about an ancient biblical story to come face to face with a woman who had been bleeding for twenty years. I was in a corner, shocked by my own image for although I am not a medical doctor, I suddenly saw myself for who I was, one of the educated ones, those who can diagnose, those who put people through a lot of suffering, but who do not actually reach out to heal the sick. Today, I find myself much closer to bleeding women and in particular to the Island woman. I now see myself as the bleeding woman, pushing through the crowds, stretching my hand towards you, telling myself that, if only I could touch your garments, I will be healed. Have I touched you? I have faith that you will stop and say, "Who touched me?"

(Musa M. Dube, "Who touched me?")

SOME MEMORIES NEED HEALING

Those who come to comfort and care for people in emotional pain often say, "Time heals all wounds." Time certainly heals wounds, but there are some incidents and events in a person's life that are so deep and so painful that the mind cannot let go of them. Those who have survived wars, rape, incest, torture, terrible betrayals and experienced brutal violence are in desperate need for the healing of their memories. The pain that they constantly carry with them weighs them down and does not allow them to live a full life. Such memories need special healing.

This is the story of Rosa who is now in her fifties. Rosa grew up on a farm in the northern cape of the country in a place called Kuruman. Her parents were very poor farm workers, poorly paid and exploited for all they were worth. At the age of six Rosa's father was killed in a car accident. He was knocked over by a farmer who was a member of the privileged, educated, rich section of society. The police did nothing when Rosa's mother filed a case. The man was not arrested, and the poor widow's case was thrown out of court; neither did she get any compensation for the loss of her husband.

Rosa's mother had to raise her on the meagre salary of a woman farm worker. At the age of eight, her mother became sick and died, leaving her an orphan. An aunt agreed to take care of her and the farmer for whom the aunt worked agreed that she could live there provided she assisted the farmer with domestic chores. Of course she had to drop out of school to do the housework, and at that particular time it didn't matter much that the farm owner denied her access to education.

At the age of 16 Rosa was travelling from Kuruman to Upington to visit some relatives when the government bus broke down. The police loaded all the black people onto a sheep transport truck that was full of muck as it had not been cleaned. They had to stand in the open truck under the terrible heat of the midday sun for a three-hour journey. Half way along the journey they were told to jump down and go into the bush to do their ablutions because there were no facilities for them elsewhere.

Rosa's question during all that time was, "What have I done to deserve such treatment? Am I not also human? Do I not also have some pride and dignity in me? Am I just like the sheep and goats to be tossed into a cart and taken from one place to another? "

She felt so dehumanized at being treated in such a humiliating way. This and other degrading memories stayed with her for many years and began eating away at the goodness inside her. She was beginning to get bitter and angry and it was beginning to tell in every area of her life.

Then she was brought to the Healing of Memories Programme. This programme was aimed at assisting people like her to enable them to share the experiences of human rights abuse and bring them to understand, realize and accept that God loves them. After being given the opportunity to speak about her experience, and several counselling sessions, Rosa began to realise that such humilating and degrading experiences were not her fault. She learnt that it was an evil system which inflicted and perpetuated experiences and injustices like hers. Rosa was too old to return to school and resume her education. She could not live a life that empowered her to do anything else other than housework. But the links with the Healing of Memories Programme and the counselling she received enabled her to let go of her painful

© Peter Williams: PhotoOikoumene

memories. Her healing came from the fact the she knew that God loved and accepted her just as she was - a poor, black woman who was a house worker. And she was happy with this.

SOME LIFESTYLES NEED HEALING

Sister Anne Grey shares this story from Hong Kong

A Ling is a young woman from Hong Kong. Born into a poor family, she had to leave school at a very young age to help her parents and to support her brothers and sisters. For a while she worked in a factory. She met a young man, fell in love and they were married. However, some months after her marriage she discovered that her husband was addicted to heroin and had borrowed huge amounts of money to support his drug habit. Unable to pay back the money to the loan sharks, who are usually connected to the Triads, A Ling's husband had no choice. He had to send A Ling to work as a sex worker in one of the many night clubs owned by the Triads. A Ling was horrified but, because she loved her husband and believed this was the only way she could save him, she agreed to do this.

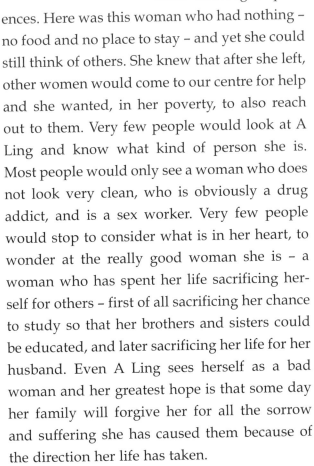

© Peter Williams: PhotoOikoumene

her friend and said, "How about if we earn some money today (and note she said 'if' – there was every possibility she'd earn none) we give some to Reach Out?"

In the 13 years in which I have been involved with the sex workers, this has been one of my most moving experi-

Life changed overnight for poor A Ling. She found it difficult to block out the things she had to do as a sex worker. As the days progressed and as the number of her clients increased, she started taking heroin to ease the pain in her mind.

> *Here was this woman who had nothing – no food and no place to stay – and yet she could still think of others.*

As time passed, she and her husband began to quarrel over the things she had to do to keep up his addictions and to pay off his debts. They divorced, so she no longer had to support him, but she continued in the sex industry because that was the only way she could also support her own drug habit which, sadly, she had acquired.

Often she had no money for food or rent, so she spent the night in the public toilets – not the cleanest of places by any means.

One day she came to our centre, having eaten nothing the previous day, and began to eat all the snacks we had laid out. As she ate, she apologised for eating so much, but I told her, "Eat them and we will buy more." She then asked if I needed to wait for people to donate money before I could buy more. When I said yes, she turned to

ences. Here was this woman who had nothing – no food and no place to stay – and yet she could still think of others. She knew that after she left, other women would come to our centre for help and she wanted, in her poverty, to also reach out to them. Very few people would look at A Ling and know what kind of person she is. Most people would only see a woman who does not look very clean, who is obviously a drug addict, and is a sex worker. Very few people would stop to consider what is in her heart, to wonder at the really good woman she is – a woman who has spent her life sacrificing herself for others – first of all sacrificing her chance to study so that her brothers and sisters could be educated, and later sacrificing her life for her husband. Even A Ling sees herself as a bad woman and her greatest hope is that some day her family will forgive her for all the sorrow and suffering she has caused them because of the direction her life has taken.

Women like A Ling are in desperate need of healing. We can almost see her standing at the well, talking to Jesus saying, "I am a woman with a past" and Jesus offering her the healing water of life and A Ling gratefully reaching out for it.

20

THE TAMAR CAMPAIGN

Today, the healing touch for many women is given by groups who use the Tamar Campaign.

This campaign came out of a series of Bible studies held in poor and marginalized communities around Pietermaritzburg in the province of KwaZulu–Natal in South Africa. The text 2 Samuel 13:1-22 is used in contextual Bible study, where the emphasis is on reading "with" rather than reading "for" or "to" untrained readers of the Bible. The readers are allowed to read and interpret the text from their own context, cultural background and life-experience. The story of the rape of Tamar has proved to be a vital resource in contextual Bible study. The aim is to help bring about personal and social transformation.

The women participants (especially victims of abuse) relate to the rape of Tamar as their own story, and find encouragement from Tamar's action in the whole drama. They notice that she said "No", she named rape for what it was. She found some liberating aspects in her culture ("such a thing is not done in Israel") even though she was ultimately overpowered and raped by her brother. Later she was forcefully removed from the house. The women observed that Tamar cried out loud, and tore her garments. This is speaking out about her abuse, rather than suppressing it and suffering in silence.

The result is that women resolve to speak out about their experiences of abuse; they find healing and comfort through specialized counselling and support groups. This text which is terrifying in some ways is being used to liberate women from their fear and shame of rape and incest.

CHILDREN TOO STAND IN GREAT NEED OF HEALING TODAY

Children have always been a very vulnerable target for sickness, disease, suffering and abuse. At one time children were protected from the ravages of war, but today we see child soldiers holding lethal looking guns, throwing bombs and deadly cocktails, being caught in the vicious cycle of hate. We see them being used to sell drugs, peddle pornography, and do all kinds of ugly things to earn a living for warped adults.

Then there are children who are victims of war, those who have stood on land mines and have had their bodies torn apart, those who have had hands and feet amputated by rebel soldiers, those who have had to watch their mothers and sisters being raped and their fathers being killed. Such ugly trauma is too much for young innocent minds.

Children bear too the wounds and scars of domestic abuse and manipulations between adults, incest, family breakdowns and betrayals. Where are they to find healing for such wounds?

We know that when the adults rebuked the children for coming close to Jesus he took them on his knee and held them close to him. How lucky those children were. Who will hold wounded, damaged children today?

COFFEE GROUNDS SAVED MY LIFE

Both of my parents were of deep faith, and it was expressed in their goodness, insight, and simplicity of life. From them I learned a love of God, of people, of animals and realized all were rooted in a beauty and simplicity of life. As a child I don't recall living in fear, except for the bite of

21

snakes, jaguars, or a swarm of insects. There were no toys, no medicines, vaccines, or antibiotics. In fact, I recall a time that it was coffee grounds that saved my life. I was riding a horse and a took a heavy fall which left me with a deep wound in my head. My mother applied a pack of coffee grounds and the wound was able to heal.

(Archie Brunn, Bolivia)

FOR SEMANA, HEALING IS MUCH HARDER

For children, hatred, prejudices, differences in faith, race and culture have no meaning. These are issues that are imposed on a child by a cruel, adult world. When a child has lost his limbs, or been raped, or has lost parents, family and home, the wounds he or she carries are so deep and so enormous that one wonders if anything can ever make life happy or normal for this child. There are many such children in our world today who have experienced the frightening brutality of violence and war and who desperately need healing.

During the 1994 genocide in Rwanda, many women were raped by rebel soldiers. Some of these women became pregnant and gave birth to children. One such child is Semana. Semana is now nine years old. He has often wondered why he does not have a father. Every time he broached the subject with his mother, she would get angry and begin to cry. Semana did not like to see his mother cry, so he stopped asking her.

One day one of the older boys in his school teased him saying that his father was a murderer who killed many women and children. Semana was shocked. Could this be true? Was this the reason his mother did not want to talk about his father? A sharp pain which he had never felt before burnt his heart. Unable to bear it, he crumpled to the ground. After a while, he got up and decided that he had to talk to his mother even if she got angry with him. He had to know.

The next day, Semana sat alone under the shade of a small tree, trying to make sense of his broken life. He had faced his mother's anger boldly. But he could not face her sadness. He put his arms around her and held her close to him as she wept and wept and soon his own hot tears joined hers

22

on his shoulder. At first he wondered, "Why did this happen?" Then as he knew that there was no answer to this, he moved on to another painful question.

"Who is my father? Can I search for him? Would my father know me?"

He knew that these were useless quesions too as his mother had said that many men could have been his father. The pain in his heart had not lifted even one little bit. It was as if the bright, African sun which he loved so much had suddenly disappeared from the sky making everything seem dark and cold and frightening.

> **Through its missionary engagement, the church's healing diakonia (the sharing of God's healing and life-giving love) reaches out for the entire humanity and creation.**
> **(HH Aram I)**

We know that children were precious to Jesus. He drew them to him and treasured their innocence. In his presence many would have been healed. Who will reach out and touch today's children?

Our needs for healing are as wide and deep as the ocean.

Whether it is a mild chronic pain that keeps us awake some nights, or something more serious, or a situation that is not under our control, we are all desperate for healing. We cry out and weep in pain, longing to be made whole, yearning for harmony in our lives. Sometimes the dawn brings relief from pain, sometimes a miracle occurs and we are healed. But most often, healing and harmony come from the loving care and tender touch of those who love us and care for us in Jesus' name.

For you to meditate

Lord of all creation,

we stand in awe before you,

impelled by visions of the harmony of man.

We are children of many traditions –

Inheritors of shared wisdom and tragic misunderstandings,

Of proud hopes and humble successes.

Now it is time for us to meet –

In memory and truth,

In courage and trust,

In love and promise

In need of healing.

In that we share,

Let us see the common prayer of humanity;

In that in which we differ,

Let us wonder at the freedom of man;

In our unity and our differences,

Let us know the uniqueness that is God.

(Jewish tradition)

For you to reflect

⇨ *In what areas of your life do you feel a deep need for healing?*

⇨ *Which of these stories did you find inspiring or challenging? Why?*

For you to discuss

⇨ *Seeing the many needs of people around you, how important is it to you or your group to address these needs?*

⇨ *In what ways can you address these needs?*

HEALING THROUGH PRAYER

Prayer, one of the deepest experiences of the human heart, is an intrinsic need for all of us. No matter what our faith traditions, prayer instantly connects us to God. It is when we are in pain that we want to connect with God instantly and prayer makes this possible. When in pain, even those who do not believe in God desperately cry out: "Oh! God, please help me," and often, much to their surprise find out that in fact there is a God who hears prayer and who heals.

Every experience of healing is personal. When one has been healed through the power of prayer, one's faith in prayer as the healing medium is strengthened. So too is the faith of those closest to the one who has been healed.

Sometimes, despite prayers for healing, one may not be cured of the disease or receive respite from suffering. This does not mean that the prayer has been unanswered. Often, even when cure has been withheld, and an end to suffering denied in the way we expect it, prayer still enables healing to flow into our heart to help us accept the situation, no matter how hard it is.

NEW CREATION HEALING CENTRE

At the first sign of sickness or disease, one is rushed to hospital. There, the doctors see to the patient's heart or stomach or wherever the problem seems to be. The affected area is treated and the person goes home cured or sometimes not cured. Sometimes, the sickness is not just in the body, but in the soul as well. Often it is the sickness in the soul which manifests itself as sickness in the body. Very rarely do doctors treat the body, mind and soul – the whole person.

The New Creation Healing Centre is an intentionally whole-person Christian healing ministry combining the scientific practice of medicine with psychotherapy - counselling from a distinctly orthodox Christian perspective and with prayer ministry. Of the medical centre patient population of approximately 1200, the majority come simply for competent, friendly medical care. A sizeable minority, however, want whole person care of body, soul, spirit. We offer this care and we offer to pray with every patient at every visit. The patient, of course, has the right to decline this, although most people now accept prayer at the end of the appointment.

LISTEN TO SOME OF THE STORIES FROM THE NEW HEALING CENTRE

Over the past few years Bob presented himself with various minor but irritating ailments. The symptoms were quite real, but diagnosis was difficult and medications were largely ineffective. "It's one thing after another," was Bob's refrain.

At his appointment last summer, the medical assistant who prepared him for the doctor said, "Bob, you let us pray with you and once even reminded the doctor to pray when she forgot to ask. How's 'the God thing' in your life?" (Note: the staff is encouraged both to ask such questions of patients where there seems to be a good relationship and also to cease asking when the patient either objects or sends signals that he or she does not wish to go any further in that conversation.)

"Well, I would call myself a semi-lapsed Catholic," Bob answered with a smile. "I still believe and still go to Mass a couple times a month, but the troubles with the sexual scandals with the priests have given me an excuse to be spiritually lazy. But I still believe in God. Why do you ask?" "I don't know, talk with the doctor about it, but I'm wondering if there might be a spiritual component to your 'one thing after another'," the medical assistant answered.

When the doctor entered the room, Bob related the conversation he had just had and asked the doctor about it. "I've been wondering that, too," she said. "So let me ask, is there something in your life that you would say is out of order with God's will for you?"

"All I can think of is that my brother and I don't speak," Bob explained. "He was the executor of Dad's will and took away more than what was entitled to him. I'm mad at him and I'm resentful because I always got the short end growing up. I know I should forgive, but I don't feel like it. I was telling my wife the other day that I need to work on this resentment, but I am not at all comfortable with the priest at our church."

"We have two chaplains here, my husband who is a priest in the Charismatic Episcopal Church and Bettie, a lay woman," the doctor answered. "Either would be happy to explore in a non-

judgmental way your anger and resentment issues. Or, if you like, we have two counsellors. I'd be happy to make the 'hand-over' to any one of them for you. And, it might be helpful if you gave permission for that person and me to talk with each other about you."

Bob said, "Maybe it's my parochial school training, but I think I need to make a confession before I get counselling." And, yes, he would happily sign the paper giving everyone concerned with his situation permission to discuss him. The doctor pointed out that the content of a confession was the exception to that permission. Under no circumstances would that be discussed with anyone else.

I was in the building and met Bob. We chatted for a bit and I explained that forgiveness is an act, a choice. Often the emotions follow the act. It isn't that we wait until we feel like forgiving. We forgive, then the feelings often follow. Further, forgiving does not mean we fail to hold people accountable for their actions.

Bob asked me to hear his confession, which I did. I gave him some suggestions on how to pray positively for his brother. His previous sporadic prayers about the situation alternated between the vengeful and the patronizing. I suggested that while God certainly could lift anger and resentment, sometimes a longer period of ministry of healing was needed. As it turned out, Bob's time of confession (and brief counselling) with me did do some good work spiritually and emotionally. I asked him to check back with me periodically to see if we needed to go further. His self-diagnosis (aided by his wife!) was that while Bob was much less angry, there were behaviour patterns and attitudes that could best be attributed to a life of being "on the short end of the stick". In response to Bob telling me this, I suggested he start seeing one of our psychotherapist-counsellors. Bob did this, once a month, for nine months. Medically, his "one thing after another," has changed into just the occasional illness.

The dichotomy between the spiritual and medical aspects of healing needs to be overcome, and "scientific healing" and "divine healing" must be integrated.

(HH Aram I)

Many people coming to the New Creation Healing Centre have stated that they feel "chopped up into components" with no one addressing them as whole persons. Others have said that while they have good relationships with their doctor, priest, minister, counsellor or therapist, these people do not talk with each other about them. At the New Creation Healing Centre we make available medical personnel, counsellors and chaplains in one location. The team members are used to coming together as a task force for the sake of the individual. Sometimes we do not know the "efficient cause" of a person's healing: was it the medicine? the counselling? the prayer? some combination thereof? was it simply the loving, caring environment?

Our attitude is, we give the glory to God and are happy the "patient" is now in greater wholeness, body, soul and spirit.

We work in educating local clergy about the healing ministry and our approach to it at New Creation. While most believe that being an active partner with other "professionals" in the care of their parishioners is a good thing, many have never experienced doctors or counsellors who have welcomed their active participation. They've not been invited to "join the team" or taught how to be a team player. We're slowly addressing that in our area.

(Adapted from a case study by the Rev. Canon Dr Mark A. Pearson, in conjunction with the WCC meeting on "Health, Faith and Healing", Ghana, 2002.)

HEALED, BUT NOT CURED.

Sometimes, even though our faith is strong and we pray fervently, our prayers for heal-ing are not answered in the way that we want them to be. Yet, even in unanswered prayer, many people find healing. Rev. Dr Chen Nan-Jou from Taiwan shares this story with us.

My son got polio in 1982 when he was eight years old. My wife and I could not understand why a child taking vaccine regularly in his infancy and childhood was infected by the polio virus. We asked the medical doctors how my son got infected, but they could not give us a satisfactory answer. We asked the doctor to make every effort to help. However, the damage was done and could not be reversed.

In those days many brothers and sisters in our churches prayed for us. "Why did they pray for my son and my family?" As Christians, they believed that God is the God of healing. I appreciated what they had done for us, for I also believed that our Lord is the one who heals all our diseases. In fact, according to the Bible, especially the Old Testament, God was considered the source of sickness as well as the source for healing. This applied not only to individuals but also to entire nations. However, Jesus' teachings, like the book of Job, demonstrate that sickness is not always divine punishment for human's individual sins, nor is it normative for God to use sickness as punishment.

My son suffered not only physically, but also psychologically from the disease of polio. Imagine a boy, so energetic, always running very fast, having to learn to walk with a brace. Seeing him like this was a suffering for the whole family. In the depth of our frustration and suffering, we asked questions like, "what did our son, or we as parents, do that he deserved to be punished; or what is the lesson that God would teach us through sickness and suffering? Is it a discipline or a chastisement to my son or my wife and I? What did God expect an eight-year-old child to learn from suffering? How dare God do this to us?"

We had no real answers. "Did my son get well after all these prayers?" Yes, after receiving many medical treatments and physical therapies he recovered, but even today he can only walk as a disabled man, more precisely, a cripple. Nevertheless, through the material and spiritual support from our relatives and friends, my son, my wife and I experienced God's grace and love in the days and years of our panic and suffering. The sympathy, support and loving care we experienced led us and sustained us and gave us hope. My son, now twenty-nine years old, finished his first degree in medical sociology and a second degree in Master of Divinity, and became an associate minister in a local congregation last August.

Often those who have faith in healing through the power of prayer become insensitive to the pain of those who are sick, or to their caregivers. Dr Chen Nan-Jou shares another story with us.

There was an experience relating to my son's illness that caused us much pain. During the period of our most intense pain and suffering, a colleague, a local church minister who has a strong charismatic orientation, asked if he could see me. I suggested we meet in a coffee bar. He wanted to come to my house, but gave no reason for his visit. I welcomed him into my home. He offered to pray for my son. I accepted his offer. As a Christian I welcome all friends who would pray for us. He laid his hands on my son's leg and prayed for him. By this time my son was ten years old, and one of his legs was shorter than the other so he walked with a pronounced limp. After my colleague prayed, he said he sensed that God had

cured my son. I asked my son to walk, and his walk was just the same. My son said to the man that nothing had happened and that he was just the same. My colleague left our home, and later on I heard that he told my friends that he had cured my son, but because my faith had been insufficient, my son had suffered again. Instead of bringing healing, my colleague brought us more pain.

> *Healing must be seen within the context of Christ's economy of salvation. Christ's miracles of healing were not self-centred and isolated events; they were oriented towards salvation.*

LET'S PRAY, PASTOR!

When we think of healing through prayer, our minds automatically go towards suffering, sickness and disease. This unusual story from Ghana shows us how people of faith use prayer even for the healing of corruption and bad relationships within heavy industry. This story of "Tema Industrial Mission" (TIM) is adapted from a paper presented by Rev. Martin Frank, Accra, in conjunction with the WCC Conference on Health, Faith and Healing, Achimota, Ghana, 2002.

The covered printing press machines in Tema immediately attract my attention when I come for the weekly fellowship: the old fashioned engines from Heidelberg, Germany are hidden under a big tarpaulin. "What happened?" is my first question. The workers tell me the story: "We didn't get any more orders!"

"What can we do?" I ask them, thinking of some action. The workers start laughing and tapping me on my shoulder because they see my worried face. "Don't worry, let's pray, pastor!" I exchange my doubts with their faith.[1]

Let's cast out the demons of mismanagement!

A couple of weeks ago at the premises of the collapsing transport company "Alu-Works Ltd." we spoke about the demon-possessed man from the tombs in Mark, chapter 5 who declares that his name is "legion". The workers were standing outside under the Neem-tree during our weekly morning prayer before working time. We tried to find out the meaning of "legion". Were not the legions of Roman soldiers destroying the country like demons? Therefore the question raised was: "Who are the legions here in Tema, which try to destroy us and our company?"

The answer came promptly: "That's the mismanagement here!"

I intervened: "How could you cast out that particular demon?" There was no doubt among the workers: "Through prayer!" said one. Another said, "Pastor, when we approach our managers to talk, they close their hearts. Their hearts have hardened. But when Moses was confronting Pharaoh to let the people go, God sent frogs from heaven. God has to send frogs from heaven against our management! So let's pray!"[2]

The prayers at Alu-Works Ltd. which cry for frogs from heaven against the mismanagement are not meant to and don't seem to replace the workers efforts. That would be a typically western temptation. One must realise that the fighting energy of the workers in Tema is limited. The rate of unemployment is very high, hence they all live with the fear of being replaced in their jobs. For a long time the minimum wage has been less than one dollar a day. Therefore the workers in Tema are very suspicious of getting any reasonable result in their favour by using the power of political means such as strikes.[3] They trust more the intervention which comes from heaven, an option which in their eyes would have little in common with the famous Marxist slogan "opium of the people".

A second remark is that the imported Christianity from the West didn't change the worldview of the people in Ghana. What do I mean by "worldview"? Our worldview is feeding our daily behaviours, our values and even our faith. Our worldview is asking, "what is real in our life? In the worldview of almost every Ghanaian Christian – not only of some Pentecostals - "real" in the daily life is the cosmic battle between Satan and God, which is also presented as real in the Bible. A creative fusion of the biblical worldview with the primal African culture has taken place since the missionaries entered the so-called "Gold Coast".[4] The battle between different spirits as understood in the classical Ghanaian worldview was slightly transformed to match a biblical interpretation of the battle between God and Satan. This battle plays an important role for the "normal" person in his or her search for abundant life "in which health, material blessings, and protection from evil powers are significant". Evil spirits often block the way to this life with both its personal success and its political implications. Therefore believers overfill the churches in Ghana that cast out these demons, to seek for health, even to get a visa. Leading in the propagation of the ongoing battle are the Pentecostals. But for the last thirty years one could speak about a kind of "Charismatization" of Christianity in Ghana, which started interestingly from within the mainline churches.

© Peter Williams: PhotoOikoumene

So why do workers and even managers in Ghana seek God's intervention by prayer and "deliverance"[5] rather than by strikes?

Christianity in Ghana is reconstructed by the people especially through the above-described "Charismatization". Christians in Ghana have retained their old and proved ways of being religious. They didn't take over the western religious dichotomy of the secular and sacred being different from each other. To a Ghanaian, "What should religion be but to include every part of the daily life and struggle?" *Obi nkyere abofra Nyame* is a well-known saying in Twi (one of the main languages in Ghana) and means "no one has to teach a child about God – because a child knows God." Only a few Ghanaian workers would consider the world as divided into sacral and secular parts, into the sphere of the church and the sphere of the factories.

The fellowships (prayer-sessions) at the factories are regarded as a means to "really" heal the broken structures within the industry of Tema. Therefore the famous processes of "deliverance" happening in Ghana are not limited – as would be seen by people caught by western prejudice – to healing isolated believers. Communities and even the nation are included. So why should it not be the case also for the factories in Tema like Headquason Printing Press or Atlas Ltd. ?

ENCOUNTERING FAITH HEALING
A mother's prayer.

My widowed mother was finding it hard to fend for us, her children. I, the elder son, one day developed a cyst in my right palm. We tried all kinds of medicines, but none of them seemed to cure me. Finally my mother decided that we would kneel down before the God of healing. After some days the cyst gradually began to disappear, and now when I look at my hand, there is just this small mark that remains, reminding me that my God is a healing God.

For the last thirty years one could speak about a kind of "Charismatization" of Christianity in Ghana, which started interestingly from within the mainline churches.

THE HEALING WORD OF GOD IS THE BEST MEDICINE

Prayer camps are an important expression of Christian life all over West Africa. A Christian form of an 'anti-witchcraft shrine' first used by

31

African instituted churches, they have now become an important feature of all churches, be they Catholic, Protestant, Pentecostal or 'charismatic' (neo-Pentecostal). Many are located outside of the big cities, on mountains or even mountain tops, and run by charismatic leaders who have a gift of prayer and/or deliverance.[6]

People usually go to prayer camps when they encounter problems. Illness, inability to bear children, emotional or behavioural disorders, unemployment, visa problems or financial losses in one's business may all lead a person to seek a solution to the 'spiritual cause' of their problem. Some just go to the camp for a day; others will stay for weeks or even months until they feel that their problem has been satisfactorily resolved.

> *Healing is an integral part of the collective priesthood of the church, where every Christian has a healing ministry, and, within this framework, the ordained ministry has a special function and vocation.*
>
> *(HH Aram I)*

The Ablekuma Prayer Camp on the outskirts of Accra is attached to the Church of Pentecost, one of the churches to come out of the Pentecostal movement in Ghana in the 1930s. The prayer camp was founded in 1990 by a business-woman, Kate Tenkorang, a mother of 11 children and the niece of the former chairman of the Church of Pentecost. She has since been ordained as a deaconess. She bought the area with her own funds and set up the camp, then put it under the supervision of the Church of Pentecost.

The camp sits on the top of a hill, on the fringe of the city. Its church is visible from afar. Around the large church sit a cluster of small buildings, a goat pen and a chicken coop, all surrounded by trees. It is a clean, pretty, and well-kept place.

EXPERIENCING WORSHIP – A REPORT

The main worship service in the open church hall, which seats about 800 people, was almost full. Women and men sat separate, so it was quite obvious that about 70% of the congregation were women. We arrived to the sounds of prayer and worship. Everybody was praying aloud at the same time, with many people moving around and gesticulating. After prayers, there was a time for worship songs, during which the large open space in front of the rostrum was filled with first men and then women dancing and waving white handkerchiefs.

In her exhortation, Deaconess Kate explained that the God who takes care of the eggs of even small birds would also care about barren women and make them give birth. After only a short speech, she called on all barren women and husbands of barren wives to come forward for 'special prayers'. About 15-20 men and perhaps 80-100 women came forward. Male and female church workers lined them up in tight rows, facing the rostrum. The free space was almost completely filled up with people. While team members stood all around them, watching closely, the deaconess started to pray for them from the rostrum. The prayer was not translated to us, but it was very intensive and loud. It was obvious that she did not just pray, but, at a certain point, also commanded the spirit of barrenness to come out of the people who had assembled for prayers.

Almost immediately, some women started to twitch, sway and scream. Whenever this happened, team members immediately grabbed

them, pulled them out of the row and wrestled them to the ground towards the edges of the free space. There, some rolled around kicking and screaming, while others lay quietly crying. We saw about 12-15 women lying on the ground. None of the men swayed or fell. One woman, lying on the ground very close to us, cried with heart-rending screams and big sobs.

One of the translators sitting with us told us that she herself was the fruit of such prayers in a prayer camp. The only child of her parents, she was conceived after her mother had stayed in camp to fast and pray.

While some women were falling, screaming and swaying, the others continued to stand in their rows, praying with great intensity, and in loud voices. Deaconess Kate also prayed incessantly and very loudly. After a while, she asked the whole congregation to stretch out their arms to

also pray for the people in front. After some time, maybe ten minutes, prayers became quieter and were then wound up.

When we visited again on December 9, 2003, the church was even fuller, with the ratio of men and women about the same. The praise and worship time went along very similar to our first visit, though we saw some women pray even more intensely than during our first visit, kneeling or even prostrated on the ground.

After praise and worship one of the worship leaders called all those who had newly arrived at the camp and were there for the first time. About 15 people came forward, again mostly women, who were asked to introduce themselves to the congregation. Then, they were led in a dance while the congregation was singing. Afterwards, they were welcomed by Deaconess Kate, who gave them a short introduction to the

33

prayer camp. She stressed that the emphasis was on scripture, prayer and deliverance.

This was followed by testimony time; altogether, eleven testimonies were given.

At least two women testified that they had given birth after having stayed at the camp. Others spoke about illnesses that had been healed, curses that had been lifted, and demons that had been driven out.

(Adapted from a paper by Claudia Waehrisch-Oblau and Martin Frank in conjunction with the WCC meeting on Health, Faith and Healing in Achimota, Ghana, 2002.)

A VISIT

In the context of the consultation on "Health, Faith and Healing" in Achimota, Ghana, Beate Jacob of the Institute for Medical Mission, Germany visited the Manna Mission Hospital in Ghana. Here is an excerpt of her report.

Manna Mission pursues an effective evangelistic programme that incorporates the provision of compassionate medical care and community development. The centre of the medical programme is Manna Mission Hospital that has a 30-bed facility with services currently available in pediatrics, obstetrics, gynecology, general surgery, internal medicine, laboratory services and community health.

During our visit to the hospital we were invited to have a look at the wards and to talk to staff members. It was very impressive for us to see how medical and spiritual care went hand in glove in this hospital: in the morning all staff members begin their work with a service held by a priest who is a member of the hospital team. The patients attending the hospital are examined by one of the two medical doctors. Besides medical care the patients are given the chance to pray with the staff members or to see the priest. So the patients receive medical and spiritual care at the same time. Sometimes it turns out that people coming with physical complaints are more in need of spiritual help than of medical treatment. All the patients receive thorough medical examination and treatment that is necessary and available. Patients are admitted to Manna Mission Hospital regardless of whether they believe in God or not. They are free to accept or to refuse prayer and the ministries of the priest.

Healing is the proclamation of salvation in Christ; it grants new life by empowering the helpless and hopeless with the Holy Spirit's life-giving power.

Millicent, a young Ghanaian nurse, tells us how she experiences the combination of medical treatment and spiritual care: "Receiving a patient who is in a critical condition, for example a woman with a severe birth complication, we all concentrate on the medical steps that have to be undertaken. At the same time we bring the situation before God, ask Him to help us. We pray, silently or loudly, alone or with the patient. And often, all of a sudden, while we are going ahead with the medical procedures, the situation changes and things happen that seemed to be impossible. Then we thank God for His intervention. And often the patients also praise God for His work. We also pray for and with our dying patients and their families so that they can go in peace with God and with their relatives when the time has come. For me, God is at work in all our medical care and I'm happy to be aware of that and to talk about that to our patients."

CONCLUSION

The example of Manna Mission Hospital shows that it is possible to integrate evangelistic work

© Peter Williams: PhotoOikoumene

into medical care without neglecting one of these two components. Being at Manna Mission Hospital we could see that patients receive intensive medical care. We could also feel the enthusiasm with which the members of the medical staff are meeting the medical and spiritual needs of the people at the same time.

In this chapter, we have looked at different ways in which people and communities use prayer as a medium for healing. Whether it is a widowed mother's prayer for the healing of a small cyst in her son's hand, or a group of workers praying for the end to mismanagement in their factory, or barren women praying for a child in their womb, our stories reveal the power of prayer and mightiness of a God who hears prayers and heals.

NOTES

1. For about four years the author has been working as an ecumenical co-worker within the Presbyterian Church of Ghana, sent by the EMS (Association of Missions and Churches in Southwest Germany).

2. Recently the management and staff of Ghana Airways held a three-hour prayer session where they sought help from heaven in the desperate affairs of one of Africa's first national carriers. All together they sang, prayed and read the Bible under the direction of a Ghanaian evangelist who flew in from London.

3. Nevertheless about 25 strike actions in the first half of the year 2003 were recorded in Ghana, involving 22000 workers. More than 40% had to do with mismanagement (arrears of salary etc.) and another 40% were for the improvement of service (from the Ghanaian "Daily Graphic", June 25, 2003). About only 8% of the working population is engaged in the industries.

4. "The biblical worldview is that life is just as equally precarious as the traditional African imagines; the enemy is ranged in a military formation – principalities, powers, princes of the air and demons. The Pentecostal goes through life aware of the presence of the evil forces just as the African does", Ogbu U. Kalu, *The Third Responses*, p. 10

5. "Deliverance" in Ghana has a wide spectrum: it sparkles between "exorcism" and "healing"

6. For a detailed understanding of the phenomenon of deliverance, and more information on prayer camps, see Opoku Onyianah, *Witch-demonology*.

For you to reflect

⇨ Have your prayers for healing, either for yourself or someone else, ever been answered?

⇨ Is there a healing through prayer ministry in your church? If there were, would you be an active member in it?

For you to discuss

⇨ How did you react to some of the stories you just read?

⇨ Many who came to the early church were healed of their diseases and sicknesses and used the power of prayer as a force to strengthen them to help them cope with life. Why is it our churches today are not full of those wanting healing?

For you to meditate

To you I come, to let go
anger and horror,
memory and fear
sorrow and sadness.
I let go
the hurt of the past and
look to the hope of the future
I let go, knowing
that my past will always accompany me
woven into the story of my life.
Help me, Christ my brother
to reconcile with the past and
heal my grief, pain and sadness,
help me to pack them away
and to move on;
taking each day in your company
travelling each step in your love
each one in trust
so that I never can fall deeper
but into your caring hand.

(Gert Rüppell)

HEALING
THAT
EMPOWERS

God's power proclaimed by Jesus Christ is the rejection of the powers of this world and the manifestation of His grace and love in powerlessness. God's healing action in Christ empowers the powerless; it liberates, humanizes and transforms. Christ the Powerful made Himself powerless in order to empower the powerless. Empowered by Christ, the church must carry out the mission of combating those forces of this world that exercise a demonic influence on society. The church is not on the side of power, but of powerlessness, not with the powerful but with the powerless. The church must challenge all acts that pursue overpowering, and support and engage in all acts that promote empowering. This implies conscientization and awareness-building and rejecting corrupt socio-economic systems and oppressive governance. The church remains powerful in powerlessness so long as it remains obedient to God's covenant with humanity through Christ. The church's prophetic struggle against violence and injustice is the church's empowerment by Christ. This empowerment is a source of healing, transformation and reconciliation. (HH Aram I)

BEING EMPOWERED BY HEALING EXPERIENCES

Every healing experience, whether it is our own or that of someone close to us, empowers us in some way if we allow it to. Sometimes faith is deepened, life perspectives and priorities change, and new understandings replace old ones.

At the conclusion of a pastoral visit to a young woman who was dying of cancer, I read Psalm 103. She had suffered greatly, and her body was now weak and fragile. When I came to that verse about how the Lord "Heals all your diseases," she stopped me and I thought she was going to say, "Well, he certainly hasn't healed my diseases." Instead, she said, "May I tell you

> *Real reconciliation is more than a political agreement; it is a change of consciousness, transformation of attitudes, healing of memories. Reconciliation breaks down the wall of hostility. (Eph. 2: 14)*

what that has come to mean to me? I have come to believe that for reasons I do not know, God chooses to heal some diseases only through death, and I am looking forward to being healed."

I had come to sit beside this young woman with such sadness and a deep sense of helplessness. How was I to minister to her in the face of her pain? But our roles suddenly reversed and it was she who was now ministering to me. Her

acceptance of her disease and the healing it brought her gave me the new understanding that dying and death were not the end. I no longer felt helpless. I too had faith that she would be healed. I could now take this message to others who needed to hear this.

HEALING COMES IN DIFFERENT WAYS

In the following story, a prisoner finds healing through the love shown to his daughter by Prison Fellowship workers. This healing then empowers him to change his life-style and be the catalyst of change for other families in the neighbourhood as well.

In Nepal, as in all South Asian countries, when men and women are jailed, their children who are under 12 years old also go into prison and reside with them. This is a government-endorsed policy in an effort to prevent these children from going onto the streets where they would be exploited and manipulated. Of course, prison is the last place in which children should grow up, because more often than not they are abused in prison. Prison Fellowship Nepal (PF) helps to rescue these children with the permission of the prison authorities and puts them into a home run exclusively by PF Nepal for children prisoners. The children's basic needs are met, including a good education, they are taught the Bible and the love of Jesus Christ. The Fellowship arranges for the children to visit their imprisoned parents on a regular basis.

Prisoner Mr K's daughter was taken into the PF Home and on subsequent visits to her father she impressed him very much by her good behaviour. One day, he said to the PF volunteer accompanying his child, "I do not know what motive you may have, but I definitely will not be able to repay you for the good things that you are doing for my daughter." That was the time and opportunity where the PF volunteer shared the gospel with Mr K. With tears streaming from his eyes, the prisoner said, "If that Jesus is your God, I want him to be my God as well."

© Peter Williams: PhotoOikoumene

A year later Mr K was released and he returned to his village located in the foothills of the Himalayan mountains. With a loan of US$ 50 from PF Nepal, he bought a small hut in his village and took his daughter back to live with him. Some time later a group of overseas sponsors of the children's home visited Mr K. They walked for an hour and a half from the main road to reach his village. Mr K was overjoyed to see these people when he understood that they were the financial supporters of his daughter while he was in prison. He entertained them with tea and cakes in a very simple village way, and began to share with the group how blessed he had been by Jesus since the time that he had become a Christian. He had a job and was resettling into normal life. Mr K told the group that, because of the reality of Christ in his life, he had since shared his new faith with the villagers and 50 families have believed in Jesus Christ. Such is the healing power of God.

EMPOWERING EACH OTHER IN THE HEALING MINISTRY

Often people working in the healing ministry get discouraged, as the work is so vast, and the results so seemingly few. Working in the healing ministry also takes up a lot of emotional and physical energy. At times, the worker may feel like giving up. It is important that we realise that we are all healed persons in some way, and so we need to empower each other as we minsister to others. The following story tells us how important empowering each other is for us to be able to live creative, meaningful lives.

A man jailed for murder lived with great anger and a sense of failure. With every passing year he felt less like a human being as there seemed to be no meaning to his life. One day there was a fight in the prison yard and he saw a small man being bullied by a much heavier one. He saw the man plead to him with fear in his eyes, "Help me, I need you." For just half a minute someone needed him. Normally he would have

just walked on by. But, this time he stopped, intervened, and saved the man's life. This feeling of being needed spurred him on to keep an eye out for others in trouble and helped him to serve out his sentence with a positive attitude.

On his release, he found that his wife now lived with someone else and that his children were all grown up and did not want him around. Again he was filled with a sense of failure as a human being. He tried to kill himself, did not succeed and found himself in hospital. There he met a monk who had been summoned to counsel him. "I just don't know how to help you", the monk said. "My own life is so full of problems. I spend my day taking care of the sick and helping the homeless find somewhere to stay. If you want to kill yourself I can't stop you, but before you do that again, come and give me a hand. Right now I just need someone."

So the man went around with the monk helping others just the way the monk did. The sick needed him and he gave of himself willingly. The homeless needed him and he spread himself out there too and slowly he became a happy man with a sense of purpose. He had found healing for the many wounds in his life through being needed by others who were in a much worse state than he was.

There were changes in the monk too. His busy schedule made him sometimes feel harassed, worn out and defeated by the enormity of his task. His new partner appreciated him and affirmed the work that he was doing. To his surprise he found that his partner gave him everything he needed – support, courage and hope and in his generous giving, healed many of his inner wounds. With healing came new energy and ideas. The monk went on to establish the Emmaus Movement for the homeless.

Both men brought healing to each other in different ways and empowered each other to do different things.

ALLOWING OUR HEALING TO EMBRACE THOSE CLOSEST TO US

Just as suffering is a mystery, so too is healing. We do not know why some people are cured and healed of their diseases and some are not. We do not know why some people are able to accept that there will be no cure for them, accept the finality of their lives and find healing for their souls and some are not. Just as suffering means being touched by God, so too does healing. It is the gentle touch of God in our lives that brings healing. We need to allow this healing to embrace our loved ones, so that they too experience the mystery.

Rev. Dr Chen Nan-Jou from Taiwan shares his family's experience of the mystery of healing and how it embraced and empowered them.

My wife was diagnosed with ovarian cancer in 1992. The doctors told us that it was grade 3C cancer, meaning that there was only a 30 percent chance of surviving more than five years. We accepted the doctor's advice to go in for chemotherapy and surgery. After 12 cycles of chemotherapy, and two operations, they couldn't find the cancer cells. As she was a school teacher, she went back to work for a year. Five months later, the doctor found the cancer cells again. After four cycles of chemotherapy again, and the most expensive toxal medicine, the doctors said that they were sorry but that even the most advanced medicines could not kill the cancer cells. We were introduced

to other doctors, to just reduce the pain. After that, it seemed to me that my wife accepted the reality that her cancer could not be cured.

She started to write something which I didn't know about until five months later. She wrote an article called "Facing the Suffering," with a subtitle called, "God is an eternal heavenly mother." In her article I found that she tried to say to our children, our son and daughter, that their earthly mother was going to leave them, but that God would be their heavenly mother with them always. From her article I could see that she was quite at peace with herself and with God. She died very peacefully some time later.

Because she accepted the reality of her cancer not being cured, and found instead inner healing for all her pain and questions, she was able to use her writing to build a very close relationship with her children and me. She was ready to see God and she enabled us to see Him too. I too was at peace and accepted the situation because of her. Her healing contributed to the healing of the whole family.

Just as Dr Chen Nan-Jou's wife empowered her family through writing an article, many others have also written about their suffering and healing experiences. These accounts bring strength and hope to many who suffer and are in pain. You might like to read some of them.

- *A Grief Observed* by C.S. Lewis
- *A Pathway Through Suffering* by Elisabeth Elliot
- *Rainbows Through The Rain* by Fiona Castle
- *Living With Cancer* by Mary Moster
- *A Pathway Through Pain* by Jane Grayshon
- *To Live Again* by Catherine Marshall
- *A Poem To Courage* by Manohar Devadoss
- *I Will Lie Down In Peace* by Usha Jesudasan
- *When Winter Comes* by Usha Jesudasan

For you to reflect

⇨ In what ways have your experiences of being healed empowered you?

⇨ What have you done with this empowerment?

For you to meditate

Lord, the wounds of the world
are too deep for us to heal.
We have to bring men and women to you
And ask you to look after them.
The sick in body and mind, the withered
in spirit, the victims of greed and injustice, the prisoners of grief.
And yet, our Father,
do not let our prayers excuse us
from paying the price of compassion.
Make us generous with the resources you
have entrusted to us.

(Anonymous)

For you to discuss

⇨ Can you list the different ways in which members of your group have been empowered by healing?

⇨ What are the ways we can use our experiences of healing to empower each other as we minister to others?

HEALING THROUGH FORGIVENESS AND RECONCILIATION

Modern research shows us that there is a link between hard, unforgiving hearts and ill health. We know that holding on to anger and bitterness can cause stomach ulcers, heart attacks, insomnia and a host of other related illnesses which are difficult to treat and cure. We know too that when we forgive, the healing that we experience triggers off a ripple effect of healing for other ailments as well. In life, it is not the big hurts or upsets that cause us to harden our hearts. It is the little ones. We break promises; are disloyal, insensitive to another's needs; we betray and reject those who depend on us. For all of these things, and more, we need to forgive and be forgiven. Forgiveness means letting go of the anger and the need to retaliate and hurt the one who has caused us pain and to be able to see this person with compassion instead of resentment or hate. Forgiveness allows us to transform our wounded selves into people who are able to rise above pain and reach out to others. Forgiveness paves the way towards reconciliation. When we are reconciled with those who have hurt us, or whom we have hurt, we have the chance to begin the relationship again.

© Edna Orteza

FORGIVE AND RECONCILE

In a group discussion someone asked, "Are there some things which we cannot forgive, which are not right to forgive?"

As we look around, there are many situations and events which are appalling and which seem unforgivable. The rape of women by those who are supposed to protect them; violence and abuse of children; large-scale murder of innocent people by armies; the inhuman treatment meted out to those who are vulnerable and dependent on us. The list is endless. It might seem that these are somewhat impersonal to us, but we need to remember that there are those for whom such situations are very real.

Deaconess (Mrs) Linda Isatu Koroma from Sierra Leone, shares this story with us.

Rebel soldiers had captured a village and were cutting off the arms of men, women and children in an orgy of violence. One young man pleaded to be spared as he had no father, only a sickly mother and lots of small brothers and sisters who depended on him. But the soldier chopped his arm off with a machete and derived some pleasure in it. As he could no longer work and as he needed treatment for his arm, the young man came to the city and stayed in one of the refugee camps. He was one of the many angry young men who roamed around, whose arms or feet were amputated, who could find no work, and who were in much physical and spiritual pain. One day, at a Sunday camp service, he heard the story of how Jesus forgave those who were crucifying him and how he forgave them from the cross. That story made such an impact on him that he forgave the man who had cut off his hand.

Many months later, while he and his friends were sitting in a bar, the soldier who had cut off his hand walked in. The soldier however did not seem to recognise the one-armed man. In fact, he came over and sat at the same table, joined in their conversation and laughed and drank with them.

After a while the young man asked the soldier, "Don't you recognize me?" "No," he replied. "Do you remember that one day you came to a village not far from here and cut off many arms and feet?" At this the soldier shifted uncomfortably in his seat, not knowing what to say.

"Do you remember a young man pleading with you to spare him? Well, that young man was me."

At this revelation, the friends who were with him jumped up to thrash the soldier who had caused so much hurt to their friend. "Don't hurt him," the armless man said. "I have forgiven him."

His friends looked at him as if he were mad. But he looked the soldier right in the eye and said, "I forgave you in my heart a long time ago, but I am glad I saw you today, because I now know that in my heart there is no hatred towards you. My only regret is that I cannot embrace you with two hands."

EVERYBODY MAKES MISTAKES!

It is in our hearts that we need to forgive. It is those who have lost much and been hurt much who often show us the way to forgive.

In the Old Testament, this is exemplified by the story of Joseph and his brothers. We hear of the broken relationship between them and how the rift that was caused by jealousy and hate was healed through forgiveness and love.

Bishop Desmond Tutu, for whom the power of forgiveness was a central force in the Truth and Reconciliation Commission in South Africa says, "Forgiveness is not just some nebulous, vague idea that one can easily dismiss. It has to do with uniting people through practical politics. Without forgiveness, there is no future."

Echoing these words, the following story shows us how to move on from pain to forgiveness to a future filled with hope.

Dr X was a plastic surgeon from a war-torn country. At the beginning of a tyrannical regime, he was removed from his hospital and his family and taken miles away and put to work on a potato farm. For years he did nothing but plant potatoes, nurture the plants, then harvest them. He was given no tools to work with. He had to use only his hands. His once deft fingers became calloused, hard and torn. He shrank to half his size through lack of proper food and sickness. But he did not react to all the cruelty and beatings he received.

Once the war was over, he went back to his town to search for his family. With much sadness he learned that none of them were alive. All through the war he kept himself alive with the hope of being reunited with his family once again; of getting his life back. Now that hope was gone. He tried to find work in a hospital, but realised that he could never operate again as his hands were ruined. While in this state of despair some aid workers helped him find a job abroad and he left his country.

> *Forgiving is not ignoring the past. It is healing the past: forgiving is not forgetting; it is rather remembering in a different way.*

As he could no longer operate, Dr X decided to do other medical work which did not require dexterity. The years passed and he slowly settled into a new way of life. One day, as he related his story, somebody asked him,

"What is it that helps you forget all these horrors?" He smiled that slow, beautiful smile that those who have suffered much have, and replied, "Everybody makes mistakes."

45

We can only live through such horrors by not holding onto them with bitterness and anger and a sense of vengeance. We all have situations which shape and change our lives. Hate and anger stunt us.

Forgiveness helps us to get past these tragedies and grow roots which are anchored in love.

The same formula is used for situations which are not so tragic but which nevertheless make our hearts hard: the little personal things which happen to us which we find hard to forgive. Someone slamming a door in our face; a colleague who walks by and ignores us; a child who rebels against us; a spouse who is unkind... however hard we try, sometimes these are most unforgivable. The longer we hold the anger in our hearts, the harder our hearts become and the more difficult it becomes to have a happy, easy relationship with the offender. The only way to restore harmony is through forgiveness and reconciliation.

HEALING AND RECONCILIATION BRING LOVE

A young girl in Taiwan was brutally raped and murdered. The girl's mother was totally distraught and in a state of profound shock. She could not understand how this had happened to her daughter as the girl was such a good girl.

A few months went by and she learned that the murderer of her daughter had been arrested, tried and sentenced to death. The woman had a deep yearning to confront the killer of her daughter, and sought the advice and assistance of Prison Fellowship Taiwan, who in turn consulted with the prison authorities where the man was jailed.

The prison authorities initially refused to grant permission for them to meet as they wanted to avoid a potentially explosive confrontation between the two. But the woman persisted and because of the good relationship between the prison authorities and the PF Taiwan, eventually permission was granted on the condition that they met with bars between them.

During the first few meetings, the mother of the girl repeatedly expressed her great trauma, her sleepless nights, disturbed emotions, and the excruciating pain she had experienced since her daughter was murdered. She kept on asking questions such as, "Why did you do it? How did you do it? What exactly did you do? How did she die? What were her last moments like?" On all those occasions, the man remained silent and expressionless. Still, she continued to visit him to try and find healing for herself through finding answers from him.

> *Trust building transforms confrontation into reconciliation, and thereby enables religions, cultures and civilizations to live together harmoniously and responsibly as one community.*

One day, as she was speaking, she noticed tears in his eyes and his face expressed visible regret and remorse. The man asked for her forgiveness. She learned that he was an orphan, brought up in an orphanage and had never experienced parental love. She forgave him as her Christian faith and the teachings of the church since childhood demanded this from her.

They continued to meet and PF Taiwan obtained permission for them to meet without bars between them. After some time, the lady wanted to adopt this man as her son. She reached out to hug him and both of them embraced for a long time and cried. He, tears of remorse and repentance; she of healing. She faithfully visited him every day, bringing home-cooked food and personal items. She talked to him about the love of Christ which enabled her to forgive him and reach out to him even though he had taken away the great love of her life. One day he was taken away to the gallows to die. As he walked away to his end, he carried with him her love and forgiveness - things which he had never known before.

SEEING WITH THE EYES OF THE HEART

Forgiveness is the key to living a good life – a life that enables us to move from the murky swamps of anger and bitterness to the fresh new life that forgiveness and healing bring. To admit that we have wronged someone or hurt them is a very humbling experience. To know that our well-being depends on the generosity of the person whom we have hurt; to be able to recieve forgiveness and accept the healing that comes from it, we too need to be open-hearted. Bishop Desmond Tutu says that both the forgiver and the forgiven need to "see with the eyes of the heart" to bring about reconciliation and healing. When we experience the healing power of forgiveness and the inner freedom it brings us, we too can offer it with ease and generosity.

When we see with the eyes of the heart, we don't just see the hurt or wrong that was done to us. We also see

a lonely, unlovable, vulnerable, hurting person, and it is to this person that our heart reaches out in compassion and forgiveness.

A young woman was very hard and unforgiving to her mother. Throughout her childhood she felt that her mother had no time for her and was jealous of the time and energy she spent at work. Grandmother, at home too, stressed how little the girl's mother cared for her, and did her best to come between the mother and daughter. The girl grew up with cold, angry feelings towards her mother and derived great pleasure in hurting her. As the mother grew older, the daughter completely abandoned her. Many years later, when she herself was in the same situation, she understood why her mother had to work so hard and spend so much time away from home. She began to see her mother through the eyes of her heart. Meeting her mother and asking for forgiveness was not easy, as by that time the mother had Alzheimer's disease. As she knelt at her mother's feet, put her head on her lap and wept to be forgiven, she felt her mother caress her head, and bend down to kiss her. There was warmth of love and healing flowing from her mother's hands. She knew she had been forgiven, and having been forgiven, she now had to forgive the grandmother who could have spared her so much sadness during her childhood, but did not.

Sometimes the person we forgive still continues to hurt us in some way. In such situations all we can do is forgive, bless and move on.

For you to reflect

⇨ What kind of acts do you find it difficult to forgive?

⇨ Do you feel that repentance is necessary before one can forgive?

For you to discuss

⇨ Have there been situations or events when words of forgiveness healed and repaired even without repentance? How different are these experiences to ones where words of contrition or remorse were expressed?

⇨ Forgiveness is the cement that holds relationships together. Can you identify areas in your life as an individual or group where you need to forgive one another and be reconciled?

For you to meditate

Long hours of ignoble pain were a severe test. In the middle of torture they asked me if I still believed in God. When, with God's help, I said, "I do," they asked me why God did not save me...

I did not like to use the words "Father forgive them". It seemed too blasphemous to use our Lord's words; but I felt them, and I said, "Father, I know these men are doing their duty. Help them to see that I am innocent."

When I muttered "Forgive them", I wondered how far I was being dramatic, and if I really meant it; because I looked at their faces as they stood round, taking it in turn to flog me, and their faces were hard and cruel, and some of them were evidently enjoying their cruelty.

But, by the grace of God, I saw those men not as they were, but as they had been. Once they were little children with their brothers and sisters – happy in their parents' love, in those far-off days before they had been conditioned by their false nationalist ideals.

And it is hard to hate little children. So I saw them not as they were, but as they were capable of becoming, redeemed by the power of Christ, and I knew that I should say "Forgive".

(Leonard Wilson)

HEALING THAT COMES FROM SACRIFICE

Sacrifice is not a popular word in today's world. It is too demanding of one's life, time, energy and sometimes money. Yet, in all our lives, we have experienced acts of selfless sacrifice which have helped to restore our souls. When we sacrifice something precious to us so that someone else can find meaning or healing in their life, we experience a sense of well–being and wholeness ourselves. This too is a healing experience. Sacrifice is the price we pay when we love deeply. This was shown on the cross, where God in Christ, because of his love for humankind, gave his only son as a sacrifice so that death and sin may never have a hold over us.

© Gert Rüppel: Ecu-Learn

SACRIFICE IS THE PRICE WE PAY WHEN WE LOVE DEEPLY

History has many stories where sacrifice made through love brought healing. In the Bible, we read the story of Naomi and Ruth whose souls and lives were broken by the death of the men in their family. Ruth was young and perhaps could find healing through another marriage. But was there any way in which Naomi's soul could be healed and restored to wholeness again? She thought not, and considered herself to be cursed. Ruth, however, saw a way to heal Naomi. She gave up her family, her home and the land she was born in for the mother-in-law whom she loved and travelled with her back to Israel. In time, both Naomi and Ruth found healing as they began their new lives in Israel, Ruth through her marriage to Boaz and Naomi through the grandchildren this marriage produced. Healing came through an act of sacrifice.

Acts of sacrifice may seem heroic, but they are never easy for usually they require that something costly or precious be given up. Often it demands one's own life, and this is willingly given because it is given out of great love.

THE LEAF THAT WOULD NOT FALL

Once upon a time a widow and her only child, a daughter, lived together. Their life was simple but good, and they had all that they needed and one another's love. One day, the girl became ill, desperately ill, and was bed-ridden for weeks. The only thing she could do was to look out her window at the tree that dropped its leaves one by one and slowly became barren. Fall came early that year and was very harsh, though brilliantly bright in its change of colours. The girl loved that tree. It was her life-line. She clung to it and knew every branch and twig, every leaf and sound as it moved in the wind.

One day, as she was feeling very sick, her mother sat beside her, and stroked her forehead. After a while, the girl said, "Mother, look at my tree. It's losing all its leaves. When the last leaf falls, I will let go too. I'm tired, and I want to die." The mother was distressed and now watched the tree in horror. She knew her daughter was slipping away from her. She was desperate. She wondered what to do to keep her daughter from dying. She had to keep the leaves from falling, but how was she to do that?

One night she awoke from an exhausted sleep in the midst of a dreadful wind storm and saw the tree. And the leaves! Suddenly she knew what she had to do. She grabbed her coat and hat and went out. It was cold; the wind was harsh and bitter; the air was damp. But she was oblivious to the weather and the wind biting her cheeks and hands. She went up to the tree. There was a low wall in front of the tree. On it, she painted a leaf on a twig, on a branch.

In her love and need, the drawing was almost real: one leaf, a bit ragged, a hole in one side, a dark rust in colour. The day came when the girl counted the last few leaves before they dropped.

And then there was just one, the one her mother painted on the wall. She watched it, waiting for it to fall. But it stayed. No matter how strong the wind, this leaf refused to fall. It clung to the branch, and like the leaf, the girl too found herself clinging to life, wanting to stay alive, to see the next spring.

All through winter, the leaf held fast, and the girl recovered and fought her way back to good health. But during that winter her mother became ill. She had caught a chill the night she had painted the leaf. She grew weaker and weaker and finally the mother died. The girl grieved her loss. After a while, she went to look at her tree more closely to try and understand the tenacity of that last leaf. It was then that she learned what her mother had done. Her passionate devotion to her daughter's life and her imagination had made her paint the last leaf onto the wall. The gift of the last leaf was the gift of her mother's strength and love. She realised that her mother had sacrificed her own life out of love for her, her daughter.

CAN A WOMAN WHOSE LIFE HAS BEEN TORN APART FIND HEALING?

Yes, for healing and restoration come through sacrifice. When a community comes together to make a sacrifice out of compassion and love, there can only be healing.

A young family was returning home from a shopping spree. Suddenly the little girl darted into the road and into the path of an oncoming bus. The father ran after her to pull her back and sadly both the child and the father were crushed to death. The young woman, pregnant at the time, was devastated by her loss. In time, she had to get back to work. Crossing the street again where her husband and child were killed was a nightmare for her. A young doctor who worked at the same hospital as she did gave up some of her early morning time which was precious to her, and went to this woman's house every morning to encourage and give her the courage needed to cross that road again. In fact she held her hand and crossed the road with her. She did this every day for six months until the child was born.

The other workers in the hospital were touched by the love the doctor showed this young woman. They saw how the doctor gave up some of her time to help the girl. Was there any way that they as a community could show her that they too cared for her? They all got together and asked the hospital administrator to give the young woman accommodation on the campus. The administrator though sympathetic was reluctant to break rules as she was not eligible for housing. The workers persisted. As a working community they promised that they would not demand the same privilege for themselves. Neither would they use this as a precedent

> *Healing brings great changes to our lives too. But unlike suffering, which breaks us, takes away our self confidence and leaves us feeling shattered, healing strengthens and empowers us to be joyful people with power.*

51

against the administration in the future. Their love and sacrifice worked a small miracle and the woman and her baby moved into the campus where she found security, friendship and healing.

THE POWER OF LOVE

No one is too young or too old to make a sacrifice in the name of love. This story from Kenya shows us how children often sacrifice what is dear to them to help bring healing and restoration to those in pain.

I was with my friend Denise, a nurse, in Kenya. Denise has opened her home to twelve orphans whose parents had died of AIDS. One day, while I was visiting, there was a commotion outside. One child was climbing up a papaya tree, some were rummaging in the garden looking for vegetables. The reason? The children had heard that two children had been orphaned in the house down the hill from where they lived. They knew that these children would be alone, sad, hungry and afraid. The wanted to take some food for them. It was December and cold. Two of the children decided to share a blanket and give one away. As they were leaving, Denise said, "If none of the relatives want them and they have nowhere to go, bring them here."

> *The power that healing brings to our lives is the deep force which enables us to reach out to others who are also suffering. Being healed empowers us to be deeply compassionate, to empathise, to walk with the sufferer on his or her journey through pain.*

"How can you cope with more children?" I asked. She shrugged her shoulders. "Most of us in this family have little time left. We have few resources. But what we have plenty of is love, and in the end, that is what matters. When they first come, the orphaned children are broken, sad beings. They are silent, withdrawn and full of fears. Most would have watched their parents die, some are sick themselves. The children in our family do little things to show them their place at the table, or give them their bed space and sleep on the floor, or include them in plans and secrets. The love they experience gives them the hope that all is not lost and soon they begin to blossom. Then they in turn take this love to those who need it."

(Usha Jesudasan)

THE ROOT THAT HEALS

When we sacrifice something precious to us so that someone else can find meaning or healing to their life, we experience a sense of well-being and wholeness ourselves. This story from the American Indian tradition tells of one such sacrifice and the healing it brought a whole tribe.

Once upon a time there was an old woman. She had many children and many more grandchildren. She loved them all and loved her whole tribe. She had seen many changes of season and many winters, but this winter seemed the worst in her long memory. The first snows had come early and the snow had fallen without a break. The hunters could not go out to get food. The stores were low, for it had been a hard spring with a bad harvest. Now everyone was hungry: the children, the old; even the hunters' hands

that pulled back the bows trembled with weakness. Everyone needed food.

Finally the snows stopped and the ground began to thaw. Everyone in the village breathed a sigh of relief. But then the snows came back with ragged biting winds and freezing cold. Everything was solidly encased in ice. The people, wearied and exhausted, tried chopping through the ice and the hard ground. Soon, the people started dying, the old, the children, everyone. The old woman could bear it no longer, watching her own grandchildren and others dying of hunger. She said goodbye to her family and clan, left those she loved and went outside.

She went to a place she had long loved, a small stream that flowed near her village. She went and knelt down and began to sing her death song. She wept, for her children and grandchildren, for all the others and for her people, the whole village that was suffering so badly. She poured her tears into the ground and cried out: "Great Spirit, hear my prayer. It is not right that the children die with their mothers and grandmothers and with their elders. It is not right that so many go hungry while so many care for one another."

The Great Spirit heard her prayer and had mercy and pity on the people. He sent the woman her spirit helper – a bright, red bird. It swooped down and landed on a branch above the old woman's head and sang at the top of its lungs, speaking to her: "The Great Spirit has heard your prayer and has heard the compassion you have for your people, and has seen your tears that have fallen onto the hard earth. Your tears have made a new plant. It will bloom right in front of you. It will have red petals that will open in the bright sunlight. They will be red, like my red feathers and breast, and they will have silver and grey lines in them like your long hair grown and born of wisdom and endurance."

She asked the bird: "I have never seen this plant before. What do we do with it?"

The bird replied: "Dig them out by the roots. You can eat every part of it. Boil it, chew on it, cook it any way you want. Its taste will be bitter, but it will keep your village alive until the other plants begin to grow above ground, until the thaws come. Call it anything you want. It will bloom only after the snows have stopped and the icy winds return. It will be enough to feed the hunters and hold you all until you can find food in the spring."

So she gathered the roots, digging them out. She called the plant Bitter Root. Since then people have dug them up and eaten the Bitter Root. And as they eat it, they remember the sorrow and anguish of one grandmother, who went out to die so that her people would have one less mouth to feed. Her sacrificial gesture eventually brought life to herself and to her whole tribe.

(American Indian Narrative)

53

For you to reflect

⇨ *For whom would you be willing to give up your time, your energy, your money, your plans?*

⇨ *Has anyone ever given up something for you? How did this make you feel?*

For you to discuss

⇨ *In all our lives, we have experienced acts of selfless sacrifice. Try to recollect some of these sacrifices that members of your congregation or group have made.*

⇨ *What would you need to sacrifice as an individual or community to help those around you experience a sense of well-being and wholeness?*

For you to meditate

Lord make me an instrument of thy peace.

Where there is hatred, let me sow love.

Where there is injury, pardon.

Where there is doubt, faith.

Where there is despair, hope.

Where there is darkness, light.

Where there is sadness, joy.

O Divine Master

Grant that I may not so much seek to be consoled as to console;

To be understood as to understand;

To be loved, as to love;

For it is in giving that we receive,

It is in pardoning that we are pardoned,

And it is in dying that we are born to eternal life.

(St. Francis)

THE ROLE OF COMMUNITY IN HEALING

Most of us live and work in a community. Whether we like it or not we belong somewhere or to someone. It is in this belonging that we discover who we are and what it means to be human. When we are loved, accepted and appreciated for who we are, we feel secure and are able to be trusting and giving of ourselves. Usually this happens in families, small groups, groups of friends and workmates, and small communities are formed. People in a community have shared values, visions, goals and interests. They also say, "I am here for you when you need me".

A community that is aware and caring of each other's needs can bring much healing to its members. By talking to each other, listening to what the other is saying, by doing things together and being together, people in a community can move forward carrying each other, bearing each other's burdens and being a source of healing for each other.

A HEALING COMMUNITY

Coming together as a community to be a healing agent is a wonderful experience. The feeling of togetherness, the bonding between persons, the shared goal, all create an ambience that is conducive to bringing healing. Often, people are able to put aside personal enmities, step over prejudices and other barriers we usually create between ourselves to bring healing to someone they care about in a community.

The following two accounts are very different from each other. Yet, they tell of the bond that can grow, and the healing that a group of people can bring when they gather together in love and care.

"My husband was dying and he knew it. He was sick of being in hospital, of the drips, the needles and the indignity of being a bed-ridden invalid. He was also furiously angry with God for not healing him and giving him his life back. In this terrible mood he discharged himself from hospital one night and decided to spend the rest of his time at home with the family.

> *A community that is aware and caring of each other's needs can bring much healing to its members.*

My heart was breaking that morning as I bathed him and got him ready for the day.

I had no idea what the day would bring. It was Sunday. Dr Fritschi, an old friend who was also an ordained minister, heard that we were home and rang and asked if we would like communion to be served to us at home. I thought this was a good idea and invited him and his wife over.

Apart from our family, others whom we loved and who loved us were also unexpectedly there that morning – Kumar's brother and sister, some close friends, a few neighbours and our helpers. Here we were, a small community, gathered together to share in the suffering of someone we all loved. We were seated in our garden with all my flowers in full bloom. The air was warm and fragrant with the perfume of flowers. The sky was a bright blue and it seemed that all the birds were singing in our garden that morning. There, drenched by so much beauty and love, we had a small service of unction – a service where the person is anointed with holy oil. Dr Fritschi explained to us that he was going to anoint Kumar and pray for healing or release. He asked us also to participate in this action. Reverently we dipped our fingers in the oil and tenderly and gently laid our hands on Kumar. This was an act of consecration.

Each of us in our hearts lovingly committed Kumar to God and asked for healing for him or release from all his pain. Perhaps the sensation of tender touch and the recognition of all the loving hearts gathered there united in one prayer communicated more effectively than words to him. For in that one symbolic act, all of us there, even those who did not share our faith and those who had no faith at all, became physical channels of a spiritual experience for Kumar. Every hand laid on him became the hand of God.

That small group of people gathered together that morning because of love for Kumar, and in doing so became closer to each other too in the process, despite the difference in faith, status and the usual barriers which separate people.

After the anointing, the simple yet familiar words of the communion service reached out to Kumar even more. After the service his face was radiant. Gone was the tension, the pain, the fear and the terrible anger that had been part of his life for so long. In his heart he had accepted that this was God's will for him and it brought healing.

(*I Will Lie Down In Peace*, by Usha Jesudasan)

HEALING THAT BRINGS A NEW VISION

Rabbi Benjamin is a friend of mine. One morning, he came to the table where I was having breakfast. From the look on his face I knew that something terrible had happened. He told me of the bomb blast in Jerusalem the night before. He feared for his family, his friends and for the people he ministered to. For a long while he sat with his head bowed. The cream-coloured prayer shawl over his head partially hid his face, which was pale and drawn with grief. His lips quietly murmured ancient prayers.

Some years earlier, the rabbi's life had been torn apart by violence. He lost family and friends and his right leg. He kept asking himself and God, "Why?" Why such senseless violence? Why such misery? Why him? For months he was screwed up with pain, hate and anger. Then finally, Ben was tired of the violence in his heart. He needed to find peace. Peace, he knew, would only come through forgiveness and a new vision of life.

He realized that all the years of his training and acquiring knowledge of the scriptures had not taught him how to forgive. Here he was a rabbi, one who expounded the scriptures to others and yet, when it came to the basics, he did not know how to do it. A difficult maze of negative emotions trapped him. He learnt to forgive by opening his heart and allowing God to melt away his hard feelings. A peace group who understood how important it was to give people whose lives were shattered a new vision of peace and wholeness brought their faith in a new way of living and being to him. They made him see how many more people would believe in this vision if he as a wounded person would show others the way forward.

It is not easy for those who live amidst the debris of destruction to see a vision of peace and wholeness for themselves. Sometimes the debris is of a broken marriage or an unfulfilled career, or difficult family relationships. Those whose lives are in a mess need others to help them see that there is more to life than the broken fragments that make up their lives at this point.

(*That We May Be One,* by Usha Jesudasan)

THE CHURCH AS A HEALING COMMUNITY
Church, community and mission

The nature and mission of the church proceeds from the Triune God's own identity and mission with its emphasis on community in which there is sharing in a dynamics of interdependence. It belongs to the very essence of the church – understood as the body of Christ created by the Holy Spirit – to live as a healing community, to recognise and nurture healing charisms and to maintain ministries of healing as visible signs of the presence of the kingdom of God.

To be a reconciling and healing community is an essential expression of the mission of the church to create and renew relationships in the perspective of the kingdom of God. This means to proclaim Christ's grace and forgiveness, to heal bodies, minds, souls and to reconcile broken communities in the perspective of fullness of life. (John 10:10).

It has to be reaffirmed what the document *Mission and Evangelism in Unity Today* stated, i.e. that "mission carries a holistic understanding: the proclamation and sharing of the good news of the gospel, by word (kerygma), deed (diako-

© Peter Williams: PhotoOikoumene

nia), prayer and worship (leiturgia) and the everyday witness of the Christian life (martyria); teaching as building up and strengthening people in their relationship with God and each other; and healing as wholeness and reconciliation into koinonia – communion with God, communion with people, and communion with creation as a whole."

HEALING THE WOUNDS OF CHURCH AND MISSION HISTORY

When Christian churches speak of the healing ministry as an indispensable element of the body of Christ they must also face their own past and present, sharing a long and often conflictual history with each other. Church splits, rivalry in mission and evangelism, proselytism, exclusions of persons or whole churches for dogmatic reasons, condemnations of different church traditions anathematised as heretical movements, but also inappropriate collaboration between churches and political movements or economic and political powers, have left deep marks and wounds in many parts of the one body of Christ and continue to have a harmful impact on interdenominational relationships.

Christians and churches are still in deep need of healing and reconciliation with each other.

Christians and churches are still in deep need of healing and reconciliation with each other. The agenda of church unity remains an essential part of the healing ministry. The ecumenical movement has indeed been and still is one of the most promising and hope-giving instruments for the necessary processes of healing and reconciliation within Christianity. What such processes mean and imply has been described in the document "Mission and the ministry of reconciliation" recommended by the Conference on Mission and Evangelism (CWME) commission in 2004: the local Christian community as a primary place for the healing ministry.

The Tübingen consultations in 1964 and 1967 affirmed that the local congregation or Christian community is the primary agent for healing. With all the need and legitimacy of specialized Christian institutions like hospitals, primary health services and special healing homes, it was emphasized that every Christian community as such - as the body of Christ - has a healing significance and relevance. The way people are received, welcomed and treated in a local community has a deep impact on its healing function. The way a network of mutual support, of listening and of mutual care is maintained and nurtured in a local congregation expresses the healing power of the church as a whole. All basic functions of the local church have a healing dimension also for the wider community: the proclamation of the word of God as a message of hope and comfort, the celebration of the Eucharist as a sign of reconciliation and restoration, the pastoral ministry of each believer, individual or community intercessory prayer for all members and the sick in particular. Each individual member in a local congregation has a unique gift to contribute to the overall healing ministry of the church.

THE CHARISMATIC GIFTS OF HEALING

According to the biblical tradition the Christian community is entrusted by the Holy Spirit with a great variety of spiritual gifts (1 Cor. 12) in which charisms relevant to the healing ministry have a prominent role. All gifts of healing within a given community need deliberate encouragement, spiritual nurture, education and enrichment but also a proper ministry of pastoral accompaniment and ecclesial oversight. Charisms are not restricted to the so-called "supernatural" gifts which are beyond common understanding and/or personal worldview, but hold to a wider understanding in which both talents and approaches of modern medicine, alternative medical approaches as well as gifts of traditional healing and spiritual forms of healing have their own right. Among the most important means and approaches to healing within Christian tradition mention should be made of

- the gift of praying for the sick and the bereaved
- the gift of laying on of hands
- the gift of blessing
- the gift of anointing with oil
- the gift of confession and repentance
- the gift of consolation
- the gift of forgiveness
- the gift of healing wounded memories
- the gift of healing broken relationships and/or the family tree
- the gift of meditative prayer
- the gift of silent presence
- the gift of listening to each other
- the gift of opposing and casting out evil spirits (ministry of deliverance)
- the gift of prophecy (in the personal and socio-political realms)

THE EUCHARIST AS THE CHRISTIAN HEALING EVENT PAR EXCELLENCE

The celebration of the Eucharist is considered by the majority of Christians as the most prominent healing gift and unique healing act in the church in all her dimensions. While the essential contribution of the Eucharist for healing is not understood in the same manner by all denominational traditions, the sacramental aspect of Christian healing is more deeply appreciated and expressed in many churches today. In the Eucharist, Christians experience what it means to be brought together and to be made one, constituted again as the body of Christ across social, linguistic and cultural barriers, however not yet across denominational divides. The remaining division between churches, which prevents a common celebration at the Lord's table, is the reason why many Christians have difficulties in grasping and experiencing the Eucharist as the healing event par excellence.

The Eucharistic liturgy provides the setting and visible expression for God's healing presence in the midst of the church and through her in mission to this broken world. The healing dimension of the Eucharist is underscored by the tradition

© Peter Williams: PhotoOikoumene

reaching back to the early church requesting reconciliation with the brother or sister prior to sharing the sacrament. It is expressed also through the mutual sharing of the peace and forgiveness of sins between God and the believers in the liturgy of confession. Very early evidence is also there for the Christian practice to share the Eucharist with the sick and to bring it to homes and hospitals. The body of Christ, broken for the suffering world, is received as the central gift of God's healing grace. Every eucharistic celebration restores both the community of the church and renews the healing gifts and charisms. According to ancient sources the liturgical tradition of anointing the sick with oil is rooted in the Eucharistic celebration. In both Roman Catholic and Orthodox traditions the oil used for anointing the sick is sanctified by the local bishop in the liturgy of benediction of the oil during Holy Week (chrismation mass), thereby rooting the healing ministry of the church both in the Eucharist and in the cross and resurrection of Christ.

> *All basic functions of the local church have a healing dimension also for the wider community.*

THE HEALING DIMENSION OF WORSHIP IN GENERAL AND SPECIAL HEALING SERVICES

For all Christian denominations and church traditions it holds true that the worshipping community and the worship itself can have a deep healing dimension. Opening oneself in praise and lament to God, joining the others as a community of believers, being liberated from guilt and burdens of life, experiencing even unbelievable cures, being inflamed by the experience of singing and of praise, are a tremendously healing experience. It must however also be acknowledged that this can never be taken for granted. Inappropriate forms of Christian worship including triumphalistic "healing services" in which the healer is glorified at the expense of God and where false expectations are raised, can deeply hurt and harm people.

In many places, still, special monthly or weekly services are experienced as authentic witness to God's healing power and care. Indeed, in such worship, explicit recognition is given to the needs of those seeking healing from experiences of loss, of fragmentation, of despair or physical illness. In many church traditions worship events combine the Eucharist with the ritual of personal prayer for the sick and the laying on of hands and are an appropriate response both to the mandate of the church and the longing for healing within the population. The contribution of Pentecostalism and the charismatic movement both within and outside the historical churches to the contemporary renewal of the understanding of the healing dimension of worship and of mission in general has to be acknowledged in this context.

DEEPENING A COMMON UNDERSTANDING OF A CHRISTIAN HEALING SPIRITUALITY

It is clear for all Christian traditions that Christian healing ministries cannot be seen as mere techniques and professional skills or cer-

tain rituals. All of them depend on a Christian spirituality and discipline which influences all spheres of personal as well as professional life. Such spirituality depends on faith in God, following Christ's footsteps, on how the body is treated, how the limitations of space and time are dealt with, how pain and sickness are coped with, how one eats and fasts, prays and meditates, visits the sick, helps the needy and keeps silence in openness to God's Spirit.

There is a need for discernment as to what constitutes authentic Christian spirituality. There exist theologies and forms of Christian practice that do not contribute to healing. Distorted forms of spirituality or piety can lead to unhealthy lives and questionable relationships with God and fellow human beings.

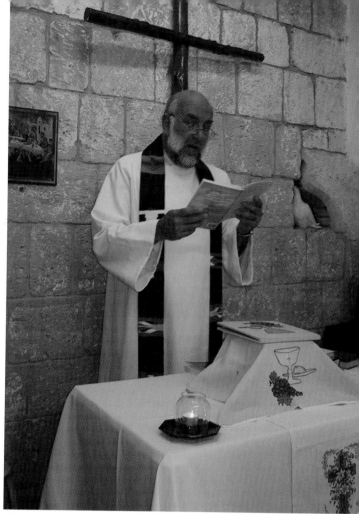

© Gert Rüppel: Ecu-Learn

THE ORDAINED AND THE LAITY IN THE HEALING MINISTRY

In many congregations it can be observed that only ordained people are allowed to extend signs of blessing and prayers of healing for people who are in need. Biblical evidence reminds us however that the Spirit and the Spirit's gifts have been promised to all members of the people of God (Acts 2:17, 1 Cor. 12:3 ff) and that every member of the church is called to participate in the healing ministry. Churches are encouraged to support the gifts and potentials, particularly of lay people both in local congregations as well as in health care institutions. Empowering people to act as ambassadors of the healing ministry is an essential task of both the ordained ministers and deacons in the church as well as the Christian professionals working in various health-related institutions.

How each church can best recognise the mandate of the local community, express the responsibility of the ordained ministry and of lay peo-

ple in the healing ministry, depends on its own tradition and structure. The Church of England has appointed in many places a healing advisor on the level of the diocese. This minister is responsible for encouragement, education and also spiritual and pastoral advice for emerging healing ministries in cooperation with the regional bishop. The healing ministry of the church thereby receives a visible recognition and support in the church as a whole instead of just being delegated to specialized institutions or restricted to the local situation.

THE NEED FOR EDUCATING CHRISTIANS FOR THE HEALING MINISTRY

There is a growing consensus that education for the different forms of Christian healing ministry is not as widespread and developed as it ought to be in the various sectors of church life. Explicit teach-

61

© Peter Williams: PhotoOikoumene

concept of Primary Health Care (PHC) in the 1980s created a PHC movement that began with great hope for change, but has not been sustained. The divide created between high technology-based medicine on the one hand and primary health care on the other has been detrimental to the struggle for a better and healthier world. While committed Christian professionals developed outstanding programmes in primary health care, the congregational involvement in the PHC movement was patchy and minimal. Though the access and justice issues were addressed to some extent in that movement, the spiritual aspects were not addressed appropriately. Traditional systems of medicine in many countries have been unnecessarily condemned by the modern allopathic system of medicine and have developed in isolation and in competition to it, creating problems of relation between Christian communities and traditional health specialists.

ing on a Christian understanding of healing in many programmes of theological education is absent or still underdeveloped. However, recently, efforts have been made to include HIV/AIDS in the curricula of institutions of theological education in Africa. But many training and educational programmes are taking place only within the different fields of specialized competence. Nurses, doctors, diaconical workers are educated within their own

Christian churches should be open and receptive to listen and learn from the situation of those facing the ever-more growing contradictions and shortcomings within the established medical systems.

professional fields. There is no interaction between different education programmes and fields of competencies, and there is a lack to introduce issues and basic themes of Christian healing within the mainline stream of ministerial and adult education in general.

THE HEALING MINISTRY OF THE COMMUNITY AND HEALING PROFESSIONS

The deliberations of the consultations at Tübingen in 1964 and 1967 and the setting up of the CMC in 1968, with the development of the

Additional dramatic changes in society and health systems have brought increased tensions in recent years for many of those who are working within the established medical systems, in particular in industrialised countries and centres. Increasing pressures to rationalise health care, to reduce costs and medical personnel, tend to prevent doctors, nurses and assistants to relate to a holistic approach in health and healing. At the same time, the need for addressing the whole person in health care has become more than obvious in many parts of the world. How medical personnel will be able to respond to these contradictory requests remains an open question. It is encouraging to discern signs and signals of a new quest and openness for cooperation with religious organizations, particularly Christian churches, in many secular institutions of the established health system.

Christian churches should be open and receptive to listen and learn from the situation of those facing the ever-more growing contradictions and shortcomings within the established medical systems.

The health professionals on their part should recognise that health issues move beyond the individual to the community, which is a social network with many resources and skills that can promote health. Health professionals are challenged to see themselves as part of a broader network of healing disciplines that include the medical, technical, social and psychological sciences, as well as religions and traditional approaches to healing. This wider view will help the professionals to integrate suffering into the concept of health and enable people with incurable physical problems to be healed persons. It will also encourage the health professionals to share information with and empower the patient to feel responsible and take decisions for their own health.

The primary health care approach in the community should be backed by adequate secondary and tertiary care facilities. The referral system should be reciprocal and mutually supportive.

HEALING MINISTRY AND ADVOCACY

While this document concentrates on the medical and spiritual aspects of the healing ministry, it acknowledges that there exists a wider definition of healing which includes efforts of persons, movements, societies and churches for fundamental transformation of structures which produce poverty, exploitation, harm and sickness or illness. The 1990 study of the Christian Medical Commission (CMC) on "Health, Healing, Wholeness", is still considered a valid guideline for that wider aspect of the healing ministry, which gained even more urgency with the HIV/AIDS pandemic. The 1990 document considers health to be a justice issue, an issue of peace, and an issue related to the integrity of creation. Consequently it requests a healing congregation to "take the healing ministry into the political, social and economic arenas: advocating the elimination of oppression, racism and injustice, supporting peoples' struggle for liberation, joining others of goodwill in growing together in social awareness, creating public opinion in support of the struggle for justice in health."

All Christians, especially those active in healing ministries and in medical professions, those gifted with the charisms of prophecy, are called to be advocates for such a holistic approach on national and international political scenes. Because of their specific competence and experience, they bear a special responsibility to speak with and on behalf of the marginalised and the underprivileged and contribute to strengthening advocacy networks and campaigns to put pressure on international organisations, governments, industries and research institutions, so that the present scandalous handling of resources be fundamentally challenged and modified.

TRAINING

Because of all these aspects of the church's mission in terms of health and care, training for medical and health professionals will be a key area for appropriate action. Congregations, and those who work in the pastoral areas too, need training on the holistic approaches to health and the specific contributions they can make as alluded to in this document.

There is a growing consensus that education for the different forms of Christian healing ministry is not as widespread and developed as it ought to be in the various sectors of church life.

The challenge is for Christians to continue to engage communities - in such a way as to incorporate the pedagogy of healing in the church, so as to motivate and mobilise communities to identify the core issues of ill health, to own the issues and to take effective action. This includes:

- To identify with the holistic understanding of the healing ministry in the gospel.

- To work with wider societies to bring about difference in peoples health and life.

(Reprint from Preparatory Document 11 for the CWME 2005, Athens. For this publication the footnotes have been removed and where necessary included in the text.)

THE HEALER IN THE HEALING MEDICAL MINISTRY - ANOTHER PERSPECTIVE

Dr Sarah Bhattacharji of the Christian Medical College and Hospital, Vellore, India, shares this story with us.

I have about 60 in-patients and 160 out-patients in my clinic each day. One day a newborn baby with a fatal skin ailment was referred to me by a specialist. The mother was very young and didn't know what was happening. I asked her where her husband was, and she just shook her head which meant that she didn't know where he was. Exasperated by the situation I told her I needed to talk to somebody in her family. Two days later a middle-aged woman came to see me holding the baby in her arms. "Why do you want to see me?" she inquired timidly. I took her to my office, sat down and talked. I asked her of her relationship to the patient. She told me the baby was her granddaughter; her son was the father of this baby. Her son was married to her younger brother's daughter (which is common in India). "When they got married, the girl," referring to her daughter-in-law, "was sickly and my son spent a lot of money, even borrowing money to take care of her. It was not a happy marriage. One day they had a quarrel, he was very angry and he beat her. She left him and went back to her family. My son then disappeared and has never come to see her since. It was then that she found out that she was pregnant. When the baby was born and she realized it was sick they brought the baby to me." I explained to her that

the child's situation was bad and that it would take special skills to care for the baby. The woman looked at the child she held in her arms, said, "Does God not know that we are poor people? Why does God behave so cruelly with us? Why does he allow such suffering to poor people?" Then she told me that they came from a tribe that catches snakes and sells the skins for a living, but because of the Animals Rights Act passed by the government they lived by catching rats now instead. Sobbing, she requested me to discharge them from the hospital because they didn't have the money to sustain them in the hospital. I offered to show them how to take care of the child for a week so that they might be able to take care of the child at home. They conceded, after a week left and never returned again.

In this situation as a healer, the only thing I can do is to share her pain; there is no treatment for the baby, no answer to her economic problem, and whether they will find her son. So I live with this question every day – "What is healing in this situation? Surely God knows that she is poor? Surely God cares for her; for the baby; for her son who ran away?" But I was not able to assure her of this. All I could do was to listen. This is also my role in the healing ministry.

THE POWER OF THE HOLY SPIRIT; POWER IN A CONSERVATIVE ANGLICAN CONGREGATION

In 1990 I was asked to "fill in" at the last moment at an Episcopal Church near Boston. Let's call it "St. John's Church". I agreed and celebrated the Eucharist and preached on the subject of Christian healing at the 10 a.m. service, the only Sunday service at St. John's. Often, my speaking on Christian healing is apologetic in a theological content. I try to make the audience aware that my subject matter is not as exotic as

they may think. I try to bridge my message into the world of what they already know and accept. As with most non-charismatic, non-healing oriented Episcopal churches, I did two things by way of apologetic. First, I pointed out that the Book of Common Prayer has a service of healing in it. I asked them to open their pew Prayer Books to that service. Most of the people present did not realize this service was in the Prayer Book. I find many Episcopalians care more that something is Episcopalian than that it is biblical. (Other denominations have the same issue.) So, first, I tried to make healing "kosher" for them.

Second, I tried to help them recall numinous moments in their lives, times when something highly out of the ordinary occurred, often in the context of worship or personal prayer. I gave some common examples many people have shared with me over the years. I cited a few stories in my own life of "God-incidences". I quoted the late Archbishop of Canterbury, William Temple: "The more I pray the more these 'coincidences' happen." I pointed out that sometimes God will plant a bit of information in our minds, information that proves to be quite true and valuable. I also pointed out that while sometimes we are turned off by loud, aggressive expressions of this "getting information from God", it can be for real and prove very helpful. In doing this I was trying to make other 1 Corinthians, chapter 12 gifts such as "Word of Knowledge" kosher as well.

During the time in the liturgy called "The Prayers of the People" I asked if

65

anyone wished to come forward for anointing with oil and laying on of hands for prayer, just like we saw laid out in the Prayer Book Healing Service. Several individuals came forward. I ministered quietly and somewhat formally.

One man told me that his doctor had diagnosed him with cancer and he was under medication. I prayed for a divine healing, for wisdom for his doctors and efficacy for his medication.

As I was praying for one elderly woman I got the sense that something was quite wrong with her pancreas. I asked her if she had been diagnosed with any illness of the pancreas and she said that she had not but she was due for her annual check up and would ask the doctor "to take a special look at it". After the service several people commented that the only kinds of healing services they knew about were the "wild kind" or "the holy roller stuff". They further related that what they experienced that morning was "not objectionable". I wondered to myself, are they more concerned that "nothing strange happens" than they are that "something salutary happens"? As it turned out, the cancer

> *I remembered how in the early days of the Church, Christians showed the love of Christ to the world by adopting abandoned babies and caring for the sick and wounded. It seemed to me that this model, rather than today's purported business model, was the model that God would have us use in our dealings with other people.*

sufferer was greeted by his doctor with the news that his cancer, "suddenly, inexplicably" had gone into remission and the woman's doctor was grateful his patient had asked for a special look at her pancreas "because had we not paid close attention we would have missed the problem that was still in the beginning stages". The congregation asked the rector to ask me back for a Saturday seminar on the healing ministry which was well attended. During the first morning break a man approached me and said, "I'm a charismatic, the only one at St. John's. I can't figure you out, Canon Pearson. You don't look or act like a charismatic but we know of at least three healings that took place in conjunction with your filling in here a few months ago and you believe God gives what we charismatics call 'A Word of Knowledge' but, once again, you sure don't look like a charismatic. Are you one?" I answered his question with a question, "Sir, if I had come here 'packaged' like a charismatic, what would the congregation have done?" He answered, "They would have turned you right off." I responded, "So, I hope without compromising the message, I tried to package what I had to say in the culture they understood and accepted." The sequel to this is that St. John's Church still looks like a middle-of-the-road Episcopal Church but is happily and intentionally embracing not only the healing ministry but the rest of the 1 Corinthians chapter 12 gifts of the Holy Spirit. Apologetics. Sensitivity to cultural expressions. "Packaging."

(Adapted from a case study by the Rev. Canon Dr Mark A. Pearson, in conjunction with the WCC consultation on Health, Faith and Healing in Achimota, Ghana, 2002.)

THE NEW CREATION HEALING CENTRE

In many parts of the world the interaction between the "traditional" medical profession and healing through prayer has found a growing interest among patients, to such an extent that even academic studies about the cases healed have been undertaken. One of those centres, where clinical ministry and praying ministry go together, is the New Creation Healing Centre. In its mission statement they describe it as an "interdenominational ministry promoting wholeness in Christ through the practice of medicine, counselling, teaching and prayer."

© Peter Williams: PhotoOikoumene

Like in other places, the New Creation Healing Centre practises its holistic mission

- by praying with patients who are open to this ministry,

- by recognizing that wellness is not just the absence of disease,

- by providing Christian literature on a variety of subjects,

- by educating patients individually and in seminar format about the pursuit of health,

- by recognizing that each individual is made of body, mind and spirit and that we cannot experience full health without submission of each of these areas to Christ's provision for us,

- by attempting to hold each person responsible for attention to his/her own health, and encouraging financial responsibility for the same,

- by offering low cost or free services to those who cannot afford full cost services,

- by striving to conduct all our affairs and interactions with patients with integrity, excellence and compassion to the best of our ability,

- and by regarding patient privacy and confidentiality as a sacred trust.

The Centre promotes wholeness in Christ:

- through the practice of medicine,

- by offering the services of Christian counsellors and advisors who are balanced, knowledgeable and who counsel and advise using Christian principles and precepts from a Christian worldview,

- by offering Christ-centred massage therapy. Our Christian massage therapist selects techniques that are consistent with orthodox Christian practice and belief,

- by offering Christian chaplaincy services,

- by encouraging continued education and renewal for its staff.

The New Creation Healing Centre also promotes wholeness in Christ by way of teaching:

- through the availability of educational literature, tapes and personal instruction by the staff and others to our patients,

- by periodic presentations of seminars and promoting the programme of other organizations with common goals,

- by encouraging the patient to listen to Christ Himself.

Dr Mary Pearson, co-founder of the centre reflects on this ministry's purpose when she notes, "I remembered how, in the early days of the church, Christians showed the love of Christ to the world by adopting abandoned babies and caring for the sick and wounded. It seemed to me that this model, rather than today's purported business model, was the model that God would have us use in our dealings with other people.

Given today's settings and way of life, how can we develop and nurture giving, sharing hearts that bring healing?

(Adapted from a paper by the Rev. Canon Dr. Mark A. Pearson, in conjunction with the WCC consultation on Health, Faith and Healing in Achimota, Ghana, 2002.)

THE JAMAICAN EXPERIENCE

In Jamaica, certain indices of social well-being are pathetic. Over 70 percent of children are born in homes without fathers. Close to 45 percent of Jamaican households are headed by women. Most of them have no spouse or steady partner living with them. Approximately 30 percent of children leave the primary school system functionally illiterate. The majority of our young men are unskilled. Since 1970 approximately 30 percent of the island's births are by teenagers, many of whom are largely unemployed and undereducated. In the inner city, and increasingly in rural areas, the majority of these young men and women are seen by the "brown" (coloured), white and black upper and middle class elite as constituting the "subhuman masses". Police brutality and killings keep us under the watchful eyes of human rights organizations such as Amnesty International. Our murder rate of over 1,045 persons, or 40 per 100,000, in 2002, places us among the highest per capita murder rates in the world. In the inner city whole geographical areas, called garrison political constituencies, are run by alternative social orders of drug gangs fuelled by the patronage of competing politicians.

The prevalence rate of HIV in the Caribbean is reported to be the second highest in the world. It is second to Sub-Saharan Africa, a land which was destabilized by the uprooting of millions of our ancestors. Evidence of family decay such as domestic murder-suicides, children left behind by migrating parents, street children, and child abuse, are on the increase in Jamaica. We have one of the highest rates of deforestation. Newspapers and television stations daily reel off the murder, crime, motor vehicle accidents and job redundancy statistics. The popular mood of anger and pessimism now filters regularly into the offices of mental health workers. Outward migration of skilled persons and of "disillusioned patriots" is a daily affair.

Healing by prayer and faith has not been traditionally a feature of the life of the "mainline" churches. That seems to be largely relegated to the Pentecostals and Charismatics where our Calvinist dispensationalist theology has not taken root. Notable exceptions in Jamaica have included the work of some Catholic religious workers in this ministry as well as the Anglican denomination that holds an annual Healing Conference. Here, miraculous healings occur.

A NEW PARADIGM AND INITIATIVE

In 1974, a new paradigm emerged, both in health care in Jamaica and in the ministry of faith and health in the church. This is called the Congregation-based Whole Person Healing Ministry approach. One of the main settings in which this started was in the Bethel Baptist Church. Here, under the leadership of its pastor and the "Whole Person Team", the model of health delivery had sought to reverse the influence of mind/body dualism and materialism which has limited the effectiveness of Western scientific medicine. Here health is wholeness or harmony between body, mind and spirit, between the individual and the human environment, between the individual and the natural environment and between the individual and God as centre.

(Adapted from a paper by Dr E. Anthony Allen, Jamaica, in conjunction with the WCC consultation on Health, Faith and Healing in Achimota, Ghana, 2002.)

REDISCOVERING THE CHURCH AS A HEALING COMMUNITY

In his book, "Psicología Pastoral para Todos los Cristianos" (Pastoral Psychology for All Christians), Dr Jorge León draws on his professional and pastoral experience, saying "I have often asked myself if the patient in front of me wouldn't be better off if he or she had not converted. Because what happened to that person was not conversion to Jesus Christ but conversion to the neurosis of someone who has had the Gospel interpreted for them." He makes this comment in relation to what he refers to as hermeneutics gone wild.

Sometimes I also meekly used to ask myself this very same question. But I think it would be useful to use such doubts as a "launch pad" for looking at the church as a determining factor with regard to health and illness and building a healing faith community; given that health is not a permanent, absolute state, rather we talk of health as being an attitude towards life, a path to be followed, a process.

Since Jesus established the redeeming community, the church has lived in a state of tension caused by the gap between the actual situation and the aims it has been called upon to fulfil "...so as to present the church to himself in splendour, without a spot or wrinkle or anything of the kind - yes, so that she may be holy and without blemish." (Ephesians 5:27). The "already" and the "not yet", however, continue to provide a model which allows men and women to grow and mature within a new kind of life, within a community of love, where the love of Christ is experienced and where together they learn to live as new people.

This is what the author means when he says: "The Church of Jesus Christ is confronted with a great challenge which must be faced, not only by a tiny group of men ordained as ministers but also by all of us as Christians who are called by Jesus Christ at this time to undertake a pastoral ministry. However, we speak of a new pastoral ministry because times have changed and people's problems are much more complicated."

All churches, no matter how small, are places to meet and grow in God: a community of salvation (a state of grace).

Such a community is made possible by the action of the Holy Spirit upon those

© Gert Rüppel: Ecu-Learn

freed from sin and being restored. (Romans 6:4) "Therefore we have been buried with him by baptism into death, so that, just as Christ was raised from the dead by the glory of the Father, so we too might walk in newness of life." (Galatians 6:15) "For neither circumcision nor un-circumcision is anything; but a new creation is everything!" (Colossians 3:9-10) "Seeing that you have stripped off the old self with its practices and have clothed yourselves with the new self, which is being renewed in knowledge according to the image of its creator."

> *All churches, no matter how small, are places to meet and grow in God: a community of salvation.*

and carrying out a ministry whose community programme is based on the model of the church provided by the New Testament, affecting all areas of life, teaching people to live according to the life of the kingdom.

THE "DIMENSION DE FE" LOCAL COMMUNITY

The Evangelical Pentecostal Church "Dimensión de Fe", located in the Mataderos district of Buenos Aires, was set up 16 years ago as a movement of renewal within the Asociación La Iglesia de Dios (The Association of the Church of God), an institution which has been in existence for 51 years and which is a completely independent, national church.

Against this background, Dimension of Faith was originally founded as an evangelical movement, holding medium-scale rallies in cinemas and theatre halls, during the time of the military dictatorship. Later on, the movement became a traditional church, nevertheless retaining some of its original characteristics. Now we have a more community-based vision and we are building a church whose doors are open to the local community and district, from a pastoral, diaconal, prophetic and ecumenical point of view.

We work as an inclusive church, as far as possible establishing Christian models of life for everyone: young people, children, men, women, the elderly, families, the sick, the unemployed, migrants, etc., without reproducing society's discriminatory and repressive structures.

Carlos, a member of this congregation reports on how he joined and was healed of his alcoholism.

My name is Carlos, I am 50 years old. I am married to Lucia and we have three daughters: Gabriela, Julieta and Agustina who are twenty-nine, twenty-two and twelve respectively.

I used to attend a Baptist Evangelical Church as a child with my grandmother, but stopped going when I reached adolescence.

Today I am able to admit that there was a time in my life when I suffered from the disease of alcoholism and that it was God who made me face up to the harsh reality of the life that I was living.

I married young, when I was 20, both of us were working, my first daughter was born and it didn't seem like we had any real problems. At that time you could say that I drank in moderation and had done so since I was very young. I only drank alcohol at the weekends and at mealtimes. From Monday to Friday I worked hard for the company and for my family. I began drinking excessively at parties, celebrations and at the weekends. As time passed, I drank heavily more and more frequently and from the age of 25 onwards, I was drinking practically every weekend, but never on workdays which led me to believe that I had things under control but that wasn't the case, as each weekend I drank more than the previous weekend.

All this put a distance between myself and my wife and daughter. Every mealtime dragged on until I had drunk myself to sleep. My wife, daughters, parents and siblings suffered. They told me that alcohol was ruling my life, something that I refused point-blank to admit, saying that I drank when I felt like it.

The drinking began to harm my marriage, my relationship with my family and both my and my wife's physical, emotional and spiritual health. My wife began to suffer from convulsions and to have thoughts about death. When Gabriela was 15 and Julieta 8, my marriage and my family were in tatters. There seemed to be practically no solution and my wife and I separated for two brief periods. I continued to believe that I didn't have a problem and carried on with my life, that is to say, with drinking.

I began to isolate myself from everyone else, I would stay at home so that I could drink, I only went out to parties where I knew people would be drinking heavily.

I drank and lived like this from the age of 25 to the age of 35, damaging my overall health and my job prospects. By then my life seemed to be reaching the point of no return.

Looking back now, I realize that I hardly got any joy out of my daughters' childhoods and I know that God used my mother to save my life.

She knew what was going on and was always telling me I should go to church on Sundays instead of drinking so much. I would promise to

© Peter Williams: PhotoOikoumene

attend but then I wouldn't go. In time my wife became extremely ill with depression and started going to church.

Later on her health and the relationship with my daughters got so bad that I started going to church, to keep her company, so to speak. That Sunday evening, the first thing I noticed was the peace radiating from the faces of the people who were greeting one another and greeting me even though they didn't know me.

The pastor talked about some current social topics affecting our country (the issue of the pensioners) and I think I heard him say that alcoholism was an illness; this really got my attention, together with the fact that he was talking about current affairs, something I didn't think the church did.

I liked it, I started to go every Sunday. After a month, the pastor asked all those needing to be prayed for in order to be healed of an illness to come to the front. I went up but only to accompany my wife because I was still convinced she was the one with problems.

It was at this point that my life changed!

The pastor prayed for both of us and I could feel that something was happening to me but I didn't know what. Standing up there I started to cry like I had never cried before in my life. I didn't know what was happening until the Lord made me look at my wife and see how sad and wasted away she was and showed me clearly that I was the one who was ill, very ill. I cried as never before, without feeling any shame. For the first time I had seen myself as I really was (and I was very ill). He showed me my whole life and the consequences of alcoholism for the entire family. Now I can say that it was then that my new life began.

I returned home deeply moved. Only I knew what had happened to me. Later I talked to my wife about it and things began to change visibly in my life. I stopped getting drunk at the weekends. Now it was me who wanted to go to church, my daughters began to notice changes for the better in the way that I was, with my wife and in our marriage. Within two months I had stopped drinking heavily and within six months I had quit smoking without going through any of the withdrawal symptoms I had heard about.

I cured myself of alcoholism (not magically, it took a conscious effort), my wife got over her depression and all her emotional problems (she no longer had convulsions). We began a new family life, I started talking to my daughters

again and, once they saw how my life had changed, they began to attend church as well. Today they thank God for having given them back their parents (Carlos' actual words) and returning to them a family which had grown with the addition of another daughter.

Shortly after our encounter with Jesus Christ, we went to the pastors and told them about our lives and experiences with the Lord Jesus and the effect he was having on our lives and our family. Soon after that, they baptized my mother, my wife, my eldest daughter and me together with some other brothers, with the added gift that, two days before, my wife and I received baptism in the Holy Spirit.

Now, in October 2003, I thank our Lord Jesus Christ, not only for having saved my life, because the way I was going I didn't have long left (many friends from that time died because of alcohol) but also for having saved our family. Meeting with Jesus led us to meet each other and hand-in-hand with Jesus we rejoined society and are now serving the Lord in different ministries of the Church.

HEALED THROUGH GOD'S GRACE IN COMMUNITY

Violeta Rocha shares with us the testimony of Francis Valeria Lopez Duarte a member of the Pentecostal The Rivers of Living Water Church in Nicaragua.

When she was 24 Francis Valeria gave birth to her first child and after having given birth she

ceased to menstruate. She thought it was because she was breast-feeding, or due to the fact that she was not having sexual relations, as her husband was out of the country looking for work so that he could send money home. At the same time that her periods stopped, she began to suffer from severe stomach pains. She decided to see a doctor who after a series of ultrasound investigations and a biopsy attested to the presence of cancer antigen (CA), that is to say, cancer. The doctors spoke to her about the consequences of chemotherapy and told her that she would have to fight, both for her son and for herself. The pain was even greater and more terrible than that of giving birth. Alongside the pain, as a result of the illness, she began giving off a fetid smell which was so strong that no amount of washing or medication could eradicate it. She was diagnosed with cancer in August 2000 and cured a year later.

© Gert Rüppel: Ecu-Learn

Francis Valeria says: I was cured at a time when I felt that death walked beside me and that I was going to leave my little boy and that God had abandoned me. I was always being invited to take part in fasting at the Rivers of Living Water Church and whenever they invited me I wanted to go, but each time, the night before, the physical pain and spiritual agony would be worse than ever and I would feel that God had given up on me. One Wednesday morning I asked the Lord to give me the strength to bathe myself and to go to his fast because I wanted to feel joy and be able to go to church. At the time I was shut up in my room because of the pain and depression I was suffering!

On the Wednesday that I went to worship at the Rivers of Living Water Church, I said to the Lord "You know that I've bought medication. I

haven't undergone chemotherapy because I only have you. I want you to heal me because my son is very little, my husband has gone back to the United States and I want to be healed for my son, not for myself, because he only has me." That day, the fasting topic was "Routing the enemy in the name of Jesus".

I had never danced before but I danced then, I felt a pain as if my stomach was being touched, then I felt at peace but I kept on dancing. I felt such a divine, marvellous sense of peace that I couldn't feel any more pain, you couldn't see pain on my face any more, only the dance, I was laughing my head off, the people there were looking at me. I was laughing and my mother and a girlfriend who were with me told me that they could see the joy in my face. God had never abandoned me, that day the Lord showed himself to me. I felt divine healing, the love of God, his mercy! I was healed instantly, within half an hour of having taken part in the worship I was walking more easily, whereas when I was ill I walked very slowly and I was bent over. The pain disappeared, the Lord healed me and I offered up the fast and my joy to the glory of God. I had the illness for about a year. After the healing experience of fasting, my stomach inflammation disappeared and my periods returned. The menstrual bleeding was very strange because the blood turned a green colour on the sanitary towels. The Lord cleansed me and my stomach recovered, there was no more smell and the awful pain that sometimes turned me into a coward and made me say to the Lord that I couldn't stand it any more, went away. Once I was healed, I went to three separate clinics for assessment through different tests, ultrasounds and a Pap test and the results were all good. The female doctors who had seen me before said there was no explanation for my recovery.

Talking with Francis Valeria she points to the fact that in order to heal her body, she needed the will to live, inspired in her by her love for her son, someone to live for, to guide and to teach how to live within God. But also, to help others, she recommends the following:

1. Trust in God.

2. Learn to wait for God's time to come. The answer may be immediate or it might come the next day, or at any moment. Sometimes God gives us the strength to accept that we must live with an illness.

3. Listen to the testimonies of those who have received gifts from God, as they give new life to the faith community.

4. The Lord heals to strengthen us. It is not just a question of fasting, if a person is ill and asks God for life, that person will receive.

Francis Valeria reiterates that it is the grace of God that heals. She interprets the fact that she was healed, first of all, as a manifestation of the glory of God as it says in the scriptures, and secondly, as another chance for her to do God's work. In her own words, "Now I work for him and I am bringing up my son to follow his path. I give testimony to everyone. I regret the fact I did not take the documents showing my diagnosis of cancer and the state of my health as confirmation of how the Lord delights in human life."

She goes on to say: Divine healing is received as a gift so that we may live and work in the Lord. Divine healing is what I received, it was granted to me so that I would have new experiences in the Lord because there are always new, different experiences to be had with him. I receive salvation from him once I repent and confess that he is my true Saviour.

Divine healing is unique, unlike natural or chemical healing, processes that involve financial costs, time, pain, low self-esteem. I received divine healing instantly. My self-esteem rose, I hugged my son and called my husband, I said to him "Come back home! I've been born again!" Another explanation is that the poor receive God's healing because of the current economic situation in our country. The first thing we tend to hear when people pray is "Lord I don't have the money to pay for chemotherapy, tests,

drugs, appointments or hospital stays." Most people don't have the money for any of those things but they have a living God. "This illness is no longer mine, it is yours, Lord!" is an affirmation which is constantly expressed by poor men and women as a part of their worship.

For Francis Valeria, Jesus performed bodily healing as an act of liberation. "He freed me from many things that were tying me down, from pain, illness, depression, low self-esteem, things that kept me locked up in the dark. I refused to switch on any lights and wouldn't even let the sunlight into my room. All I did was take sleeping pills whilst my son was being looked after by a young girl. That was what caused me the most pain. Now I spend 24 hours a day with God." Certain biblical texts were fundamental for her, for example, the woman with the issue of blood, Jairus' daughter, the faith of the Canaanite woman, Isaiah 44, or when the Lord tells Peter that he has little faith. These texts taught her that it is through having faith that we see God's glory.

Healing is a sign of the Kingdom of God, because the Lord's word says that in his presence there will be neither death, nor lamentation, nor pain. This is a sign of power because we see that the Lord is great in any illness or situation with which his sons and daughters are faced. The church is also a healing community. Francis Valeria received healing in a church where the word of God is heard, where the soul is healed, where people are liberated from many things and testimony is given, where faith is strengthened and where those who come for the first time see how the Lord delights in healing, in liberation and how the Lord grants gifts in many forms because he also heals wounds of the heart

© Gert Rüppel: Ecu-Learn

and soul. The family circle plays a very important role; both Francis Valeria's mother and a female friend participated in the healing process. Her mother fasted for a long period to gain this gift of healing and Francis Valeria's love for her son gave her the will to continue living.

Bodily healing is bestowed along with other blessings. According to Francis Valeria, bodily health is not bestowed on its own but alongside other blessings which benefit the whole family. The fact that she is able to affirm her self-esteem as a woman who can fully express her sexuality is a sign of security and stability. Her husband returned from the United States to be with his family, found work and the family now have their own house with everything they need and the Lord has blessed their table, their work and their family.

This experience of God also led to a concern for the healing of the Nicaraguan people who are greatly in need of our prayers, our witness to the word of God, bearing good witness as Christians and the need to educate our sons and daughters to value that which the Lord has given us as a nation, learning to look after natural resources, water, trees, animals and contributing to the education of the community to which we belong.

Francis also now plays a leading role at her local church where she was healed and where she holds days of fasting and prayer on Saturdays and worships on Wednesdays. She states that she also received the gift of praying for the sick and that she is ready to go wherever the Lord directs her, to pray for anyone, be it for healing or restoration. She bears witness that some people have been healed through her intercession with the Lord and through her laying on of hands and her testimony of her experience of healing from uterine cancer has been heard in a variety of churches. I was given permission by her to share this testimony with you here today and she hopes that your lives will be blessed by having heard it.

> *Healing is a sign of the Kingdom of God, because the Lord's word says that in his presence there will be neither death, nor lamentation, nor pain.*

CONCLUSIONS BY VIOLETA

I have come across other cases involving the same affirmation "You must believe if you are to receive a healing response from God!" This idea is shared by brothers and sisters of traditional and historic churches and pentecostal churches alike. There have even been some testimonies from the charismatic movement of the Roman Catholic Church. More than any other religious congregation that I know of in Nicaragua, the Evangelical-Pentecostal communities are those which have a real healing ministry to the sick.

When examining Francis' testimony for the purpose of theological reflection, I feel it appropriate to adopt an ecofeminist focus, employing a holistic approach which covers all aspects of our relationships. I picked her testimony because it touches on such sensitive aspects as sexuality, the meaning of life, the human body, self-esteem, the whole experience of being a woman in a world wracked with pain, asymmetry, responsibility for sons and daughters, etc. Francis' healing experience reveals a God concerned for our bodies and all that is related to them. This bodily dimension is not divorced from feelings, love, sexuality, fully taking part in life, even given the risks that this implies.

Francis reminded me that this opportunity to live anew does not of course eliminate death which could arrive at any moment. However, for humans and for the very poorest, the possibility of in some way bringing life in abundance closer represents good news, affirms their human dignity and invites them to take part in a dynamic of life that is both complex and hopeful.

Francis' experience challenges me to continue developing a theology of God's grace and human solidarity which invites us to take part in a healthy world, a healthy economy, a healthy environment, the lives of healthy men and women recreated in the restoration of relationships, because God's healing grace is also liberating. It is precisely this potential for liberation that offers us the hope of a just world and it is this struggle for life on the part of the most disadvantaged in the system which fuels the mission of the Lord's church. I believe that theories of liberation are inspired and challenged by these testimonies which reaffirm that healing and salvation are integral experiences which all may live through. Woman who affirm their bodies, their sexuality and their participation in the world as leaders, who speak up and fight for their right to live in dignity, also reaffirm their self-esteem and their faith.

In the last few years I have come across a lot of cases of women with cancer, I have seen how difficult the process of medical treatment is and I have shared the suffering and hopes of some of these women. Many of these cases could have been caught in time if the women involved had had access to the necessary medical services and tests. In other cases, an incorrect medical diagnosis led to delays in treating cancer, with tragic consequences. On the other hand, many women who are active in the ecclesiastical or political sphere, or seeking to survive, do not look after their bodies and the consequences can be fatal. That is why any theological reflection must include a preventative approach, involving taking care of one's body. This aspect, which is probably very rational, is important in carrying out this healing ministry and is something which needs to continue.

THE GIFT OF THE EUCHARIST IN HEALING

An elderly lady shared an incident from her life. As a young girl she was very close to her aunt and loved her deeply. Then there was a family quarrel and the girl stopped speaking to her aunt. Not speaking developed into deep anger and then into intense dislike. Almost a decade later, she had forgotten what the incident that led to her hate was.

One Sunday as she knelt at the altar in church, she was horrified to find her aunt beside her. She noticed that the priest serving the bread and wine was at the other end of the railing. She sneaked a look at her aunt and found that she looked frail and so very like her mother who had passed away a long time ago. Angry feelings churned up within her again. This aunt had not even come for her mother's funeral. Then, anger gave way to unease. Could she celebrate and partake of the bread and wine feeling this way? No, she could not. She felt she really ought to get up and walk away and hold on to her hate. The priest came closer. She took a deep breath and arose to stand. At that moment, her aunt reached out for her, embraced her, held her close and forced her to remain kneeling. In a state of shock, her hand stretched out, just then the priest placed the wafer of bread into her extended hand.

Her eyes filled with tears as she related the story to me. "I still don't know if it was the embrace or the body of Christ that brought me healing," she said.

Henri Nouwen, Catholic writer-priest, says that community is essentially a quality of the heart. It grows from the spiritual knowledge that we are not here for ourselves but for one another. Communion of the heart happens through the way we look at each other, our tone of voice, our facial expressions and gestures towards each other, as well as the things we say and do to foster respect, trust and friendship. If the essence of community is a quality of the heart, we need to ask ourselves individually and collectively, "Given today's settings and way of life, how can we develop and nurture giving, sharing hearts that bring healing?"

"How can we nurture within ourselves a sense of responsibility for those weaker than us?"

© Gert Rüppel: Ecu-Learn

For you to reflect

⇨ Have you ever been part of a healing experience that involved a community?

⇨ Has the Eucharist or a worship service, or a Bible study or fellowship meeting ever brought healing to you?

For you to meditate

Lord, we believe that you have called us together to broaden our experience of you and each other. We believe that we have been called to help in healing the wounds of society and in reconciling people to each other and to God. Help us as individuals or together, to work in love for peace and healing and never to lose heart.

(Corymeela Community prayer)

For you to discuss

⇨ How does your church view healing ministries?

⇨ Are you part of the healing medical ministry? How do you see your role as a healer here?

THE NEED IN ALL CREATION FOR HEALING

Who has not marvelled over a beautiful sunrise or sunset, meadows, lakes, sea shores or the beauty of silence and colours of the desert? Who has not sat outside one moonlit night and wondered what we are in relation to all of Creation?

Sadly, all our reflections have not kept us from destroying much of Creation. Who has not been threatened by destructive heat, destroying crops, drying out water resources, increasing desertification. Or by violent storms, floods, increased pollution leading to respiratory illnesses and increasing numbers of pandemic diseases?

In our selfishness and greed, we have broken the harmony with which we once lived with the Earth. When we plunder the Earth's resources, pollute her rivers, seas and air and kill the wild life that make the Earth their home, we cause untold pain and suffering for the Earth. Healing for the Earth and all Creation requires that we re-establish the harmony with which we were first created.

THE LINK BETWEEN HUMANKIND AND THE EARTH

Many creation stories have a special link between the ground (the Earth) and humans. In the Bible we read that God took dust from the ground to make the first man and here is our first link with the Earth. Knowing that the very ground we walk on is the material which God used to create humankind should make it sacred for us.

Astronaut James Irwin who travelled to the moon in Apollo 15 in July 1971 writes, "The Earth reminded us of a Christmas tree ornament hanging in the blackness of space. As we got farther and farther away, it diminished in size. Finally it shrank to the size of a marble, the most beautiful marble you can imagine. That beautiful, warm, living object looked so fragile, so delicate, that if you touched it with a finger it would crumble and fall apart. Seeing this has to change men and women, make men and women appreciate the creation of God and the love of God."

Sadly, it doesn't do so for many people today.

Author Henri Nouwen says that seeing the Earth, our home, as a precious little gem that needs care and protection is a deeply mystical experience that can only be captured by words such as *grace* and *responsibility*.

The Bishnois are a tribe who live in Rajasthan, in India. Rajasthan is a desert area and not as green as other parts of India. The Bishnois have a close relationship with the Earth. Centuries ago, the ruler of Rajasthan sent some men to cut wood. The Bishnois could not bear to see that which gave them life being destroyed. So each of them put their arms around a tree and hugged it. Some of them were killed, but the trees were saved.

Centuries later, the same thing happened in the Himalayan mountains. The Chipko women, who were tribal people, also hugged trees that were destined for the woodcutters' axe to save them from destruction. All over the world we hear similar stories of women who protect trees with their lives because they see it as their responsibility to do so.

Our planet Earth is known as the watery planet. Yet, little pure water is available in many parts of the world. Richer nations, companies that exploit the poor, and those in power, think nothing of polluting the seas and rivers. Lack of clean water leads to disease, sickness and death. The air, which is so vital to life, is also polluted.

This too leads to many diseases and suffering. We know that our greed and lust for power and domination have eradicated many of the animals and birds which God created for His and our pleasure.

We need to remember that it is because we groan, that Nature and the Earth also groan. When we reflect on healing, we need also to think of the healing of all of Creation and the Earth which is groaning not just with our pain, but also with the pain we inflict on her.

HEALTH CARE FOR CREATION

For the creation waits with eager longing for the revealing of the children of God; for the creation was subjected to futility, not of its own will but by the will of the one who subjected it, in hope that the creation itself will be set free from its bondage to decay and will obtain the freedom of the glory of the children of God. We know that the whole creation has been groaning in labour pains until now, and not only the creation, but we ourselves, who have the first fruits of the Spirit, groan inwardly while we wait for adoption, the redemption of our bodies. For in hope we were saved. Now hope that is seen is not hope. For who hopes for what is seen? But if we hope for what we do not see, we wait for it with patience. (Rom 8:19-25)

© Gert Rüppel: Ecu-Learn

Paul reminds us in this passage that it is not we who will save or even heal creation, but like us creation is waiting for the redemption of all through God's intervening grace. But that still means that the children of God should be aware of their being entrusted with stewardship, as it is told in many of the stories of Jesus. (Lk. 19:11-24; Mt.25:1-30)

> *The brokenness of God's creation, caused by human transgression, needs to be healed. In the context of restoration of the humanity-God relationship, creation has an important place.*

As we observe creation and the interaction therein of humankind, we cannot but notice the brokenness of it and the brokenness of the relations of humankind with what might be called the household of humanity.

"Healing is reinstating a right relationship with creation. It affirms the goodness of God's creation by being in harmony with the natural environment. The creation is the household of humanity. As God's own work, creation belongs to Him and is given to humanity to be used only for the Creator's purpose and glory. The misuse or abuse of creation by human beings is a sin against God. The brokenness of God's creation, caused by human transgression, needs to be healed. In the context of restoration of the humanity-God relationship, creation has an important place. It also plays a significant part in community building."

(HH Aram I)

Health care for Creation is different from what we have in mind when talking about healing for humankind. The following story should make us reflect on what it means to act for the healing of all things created.

Greenpeace has become a widely known organisation of people who undergo great personal sacrifice to raise awareness on issues pertinent to the destruction of a holistic relationship between humankind and its environment (creation). One of the concerns they campaign for is the growing use of tissue products (such as toilet paper, facial tissues, napkins and paper towels), of a company producing them from the resources of some of the oldest forests in Canada instead of using recycled resources. The area where they log contains regions where there are 180-year old forests, the habitat of species such as grizzly and black bears, woodland caribou, wolves, bald

Shibashi, an ancient Chinese practice of nature-oriented movements, attunes the body to the rhythm of nature, producing an energizing effect. The traditional belief is that healing and health are actual effects of balance in the flow of energy that are affected from within and outside the human body.

eagles and boreal owls. Much of the logging is done in a "clear-cut" method, where most if not all of the trees are removed from an area of forest. What is left behind is a barren landscape that can no longer support wildlife species.

Can one stop such practices? Groups such as Greenpeace, and others around the world, not only enter into spectacular actions, like chaining themselves to trees to prevent logging, but also call for reflective consumer action like not buying the products in question or boycotting them.

In the churches, one of the wider known activities related to apartheid was the movement, which started from a small group of German women who decided to boycott the products of South Africa as long as the government practised apartheid.

The movement grew, and *"Do not buy the fruits of apartheid"* became an integral part of the world-wide struggle to restore the dignity of black people in South Africa and elsewhere.

Today, many environmental groups use the same tactic and urge people who care about the wounds of Creation not to use certain products. "When the buying stops, the killing does too", is a popular slogan to preserve endangered species.

Philosophers like Meister Eckhart, Birgitta of Sweden and others, all Christian mystical thinkers, have for long reflected on a holistic understanding of humankind's relationship within the created world. Their experiences bring us directly into relationship with Creation-centred spiritual traditions that give evidence to a spontaneous experience of the unity of the world in its intrinsic cosmic web of compassionate interrelationship.

"God is infinite in his simplicity, and simple in his infinity. Therefore he is everywhere and is everywhere complete. God is in the innermost part of each and every thing."

(Meister Eckhart)

HEALING AND CULTURE

The way health and healing are defined, sickness and illness explained, depends largely on culture and conventions. In ecumenical mission circles, culture is usually understood in a wide sense, including not only literature, music and arts, but values, structures, worldview, ethics, as well as religion.

It is in particular the combination of religion, worldview and values that impacts people's specific understanding of and approach to healing. Since culture varies from continent to continent and from country to country or even within countries and groups of people, there is no immediate universal common understanding of the main causes of sickness and illness or of any evil affecting humans.

There are cultures in which supernatural beings are seen as the real ultimate causative agents for ill-health, particularly in mental disorders. In such worldviews, people go to traditional healers and religious specialists for exorcism and deliverance from evil spirits and demons. Only then can they have the guarantee that the ultimate cause of their suffering has been dealt with. This would not exclude parallel treatments of symptoms with herbs, traditional or industrially manufactured drugs.

Masses of people integrate popular religious beliefs and culture in their understanding of health and healing. We may call this popular religiosity and belief in health. This belief may involve veneration of saints, pilgrimages to shrines, and use of religious symbols such as oil and amulets to protect people from evil spirits or evil intentions that harm people.

Others, in particular Asian cultures, also point to the importance of harmony within the human body as the necessary pre-condition for a person's health, well-being and healing. *Shibashi*, an ancient Chinese practice of nature-oriented movements, attunes the body to the rhythm of nature, producing an energizing effect. The traditional belief is that healing and health are actual effects of balance in the flow of energy that are affected from within and outside the human body. The clogging of centres of energy *(chakras)* or obstruction in the flow of energy causes illness. Acupuncture or finger pressure are other modalities of balancing the flow of energy.

Out of different worldviews, culture-specific medical sciences and systems developed in some of the major civilisations of the world. In particu-

© Gert Rüppel: Ecu-Learn

© Gert Rüppel: Ecu-Learn

© Peter Williams: PhotoOikoumene

83

lar since the Enlightenment, these were disregarded by the Western medical establishment, but are now again increasingly considered worthy alternatives for the treatment of specific illnesses.

As a result of advances in medical science and of intercultural exchanges, some people, in particular in Western contexts, develop new lifestyles emphasising walking, jogging, aerobic exercise, healthy diet, yoga and other forms of meditation, massage and going to sauna and spa as a way to achieve wellness, health and healing. These may well bring relief from stressful situations and some chronic illnesses like cardiovascular diseases and diabetes mellitus.

> *"God is infinite in his simplicity and simple in his infinity. Therefore he is everywhere and is everywhere complete. God is in the innermost part of each and every thing."*
> *(Meister Eckhart)*

Certain forms of nature-centred religiosity and indigenous and emerging secular cultures also point to the relationship between cosmology or ecology and health and healing. There is a growing, however still insufficient, awareness of the importance of linking ecology and health. The determinants of health are clean water and air and a safe space for all living creatures. Deforestation has profoundly damaged the water supply, polluted the air, and destroyed the habitats of many living creatures turning them into "pests" and creating ill-health among human beings and other elements of Creation.

Very close associations of animals and human beings are now the cause of new forms of epidemics such as the emergence of Avian flu, a severe and potentially fatal viral infection that is transferred from ducks and chickens to human beings. The tsunami event and post-tsunami situation highlight the importance of taking care not only of human beings but of the whole of creation and of attuning oneself to the rhythm of nature.

(From Preparatory Paper No 11, CWME – Athens: The Healing Mission of the Church, section 15-22)

THE NEW VISION

We need to remember that all of creation belongs together in the arms of its Creator.

The final vision is that not only will all men and women recognise that they are brothers and sisters and come together in harmony, but so will all of Creation.

> The wolf will live with the lamb,
> The leopard will lie down with the goat,
> The calf and the lion and the yearling together,
> And a little child will lead them.
>
> (Isaiah 11: 6)

We need to keep this vision alive and pass it on to every generation. This is very important for, long before Jesus was born, the prophet Isaiah had a vision of Christ's unifying work of salvation. Then, years after the death of Jesus, the disciple John had a similar vision when he wrote about "a new heaven and a new earth". Since

© Gert Rüppel: Ecu-Learn

then, many others have had visions of wholeness and healing for all of Creation.

This is because this vision of harmony is one of the deepest longings of our human heart. And when we are the victims of that which is destructive and causes divisions and pain and suffering, this vision of harmony is a truth we can cling to and work towards. This vision of harmony also brings healing for it gives us courage when we are beaten, and hope when we feel like giving up because all seems lost. It is the vision of harmony that enables us to live a full and creative life.

One of my favourite creation myths is from the Jewish Cabbalistic tales.

In the beginning, the world as we know it begins with an emanation of light from Or Ein Sof, the Source of all goodness and wholeness. Somehow, there is an accident to the vessel containing this light. Light shatters into millions of little pieces and is scattered all over the universe – into every created being and thing. Unfortunately we cannot see these bits of light as they are hidden deep inside every being. It is said that the wholeness and goodness of the world can be restored again by each person as he or she uncovers the hidden light in others.

I like this story for many reasons. It is a story of hope. It tells us that our world can be restored to its original goodness and wholeness and that the restoration depends on relationships and acts of service not only to each other, but to all of creation.

(That We May Be One, by Usha Jesudasan)

Healing is reinstating a right relationship with creation. It affirms the goodness of God's creation by being in harmony with the natural environment. The creation is the household of humanity. As God's own work, creation belongs to Him and is given to humanity to be used only for the Creator's purpose and glory.

For you to reflect

⇨ Have you ever experienced a personal link between you and the Earth which gave you a sense of responsibility for healing it?

⇨ Which of our destructive ways has made a deep impact on you?

For you to discuss

⇨ Health care for Creation could very well be just a slogan. Can you think of ways of making this a reality in your community?

⇨ As a group can you think of ways of passing on the new vision?

For you to meditate

O Lord, you have wrought this great world with exceeding beauty.

Let there be nothing in our thoughts or actions that will mar that beauty.

Where we can, enable us to replace selfishness with imagination and generosity, roughness with gentleness, halftruths with your shining truth.

Save us from the temptation to seek gain without service,

And excitement without considering the cost to others.

Enable us to stand for the difficult right against the easy wrong,

And the constructive plan that builds all life,

Rather than that which undermines and destroys.

Let your will be done more and more in each of us and in all of Creation.

(Rita F. Snowden)

APPENDIX

**PASTORAL GUIDELINES
ON HEALING MINISTRIES
IN LOCAL CONGREGATIONS
AND HEALTH SERVICES**

15 KEY POINTS FOR ORIENTATION

Paper written in conjunction
with the WCC Conference
on Health, Faith and Healing,
Achimota, Ghana, 2002,
by Dr Dietrich Werner, Hamburg, Breklum

PASTORAL GUIDELINES ON HEALING MINISTRIES IN LOCAL CONGREGATIONS AND HEALTH SERVICES

15 KEY POINTS FOR ORIENTATION

1. The longing for healing today

A primary focus of religious expectations in the 21st century is the multidimensional longing for healing of body and soul, of spirit and mind, of personal and social relations, of political and ecological dimensions in this broken world. Deterioriating health standards, the HIV/AIDS pandemic and the growing vulnerability of the human body, underline the urgency of addressing the missionary challenge of global longing for healing. The number of persons suffering from depression, from mental disturbances, from loneliness and burn-out syndromes is dramatically on the increase as people are unable to cope any longer with the general acceleration of constant changes, increasing demands and growing insecurity in their personal life situations. Those churches which address this longing for healing in their religious life are growing worldwide. The rediscovery, the encouragement and deliberate training of the healing gifts or healing charismata within the Christian community are therefore of crucial importance for the future of Christianity everywhere, including in the West.

2. Healing as an implicit theme of new religious movements

Healing by the spirit or by other religious means has become a primary object also of non-Christian religious trends and movements. The longing for healing is finding its expression also in circles quite distant from any tradition-based Christian world of symbols and convictions. "Spiritual healing" – though understood in quite different terms – is an important subject not only in Africa, Asia, Latin America or the Pacific, but very much also in Western countries or North America. It is a missionary task of the church to enter into a serious, listening and critical dialogue with the search for healing, even where it is unfolding itself in unexpected ways outside the boundaries of the church. The church in mission should avoid addressing that question by just rejecting everything that is expressed in these sometime esoteric trends. "Discern and keep what is good."

3. The promise of immediate and complete healing – temptations of theological reductionism and simplifications

There are groups, persons and even churches which "sell" Christian faith like a direct therapeutic tool and effective drug. Promises are made affirming that whoever believes with sincerity will less often suffer from diseases, will live longer and is less likely to die from a heart attack. Of course, there is empirical evidence that committed Christian faith (or other religious convictions) can have an impact on the health situation of human beings. The relation between Christian faith in particular and personal health cannot however be put in such simplistic terms, bypassing the realities of suffering and unexplainable diseases also occurring with believing Christians. Christian faith as such does not eliminate illness and suffering, but changes our attitude to coping with them. In so doing, Christian faith can have a real healing and even curing impact. But not automatically.

4. Overcoming the dichotomy between the spiritual and the physical in the healing process

Although in their history religious faith and healing have deep interrelations, the development of the modern medical system has led to a practice and perception which to a large degree reinforce a dichotomy between the spiritual and the physical dimension of the human being. The neglect of the spiritual dimension of the healing process in hospitals and health service centres is both to the disadvantage of the patients and also of the medical system. Increasing the interaction and mutual cooperation between spiritual or pastoral and medical approaches in dealing with health issues is an urgent demand of our time. This has immediate implications for the complementarity in which the different disciplines could and should work together in Christian hospitals and health care services in local congregations.

5. The church as healing community - Healing as a fundamental task within the missionary vocation of the church

Following the ministry of Christ, the church cannot but delegate the task of healing (in particular the mandate to cure) to the medical system. From its earliest beginning the church had however its own vocation to contribute to the healing of persons, of societies as well as the whole of creation. Healing is primarily a vocation of the whole Christian community. Specialised persons and ministries receive their meaning and right place as part of the healing task when they are called for and commissioned by the local church. The Christian community is in itself a healing community as it brings people before God in prayer, cares for people suffering from diseases, blesses and anoints people bowing under different burdens, accepts people with disabilities or special diseases and offers to each one to participate in its life according to his or her needs and abilities. Jesus proclaimed the kingdom of God in his sayings, in his parables, in prayer and in healing miracles. The command to his followers to pray for the coming of the kingdom (Matthew 6:10) and to heal the sick (Luke 9:1-6; Matthew 10:7) remains valid as a unique and indispensable component in the missionary vocation of the church. The disciples healed the sick, healing took place in the early Church, and all along the mission history. This healing ministry is carried out until today in a variety of different ways in local congregations as well as in special health-related institutions and movements.

6. Complementary nature of different approaches to healing

Early ecumenical documents such as the report from a consultation in Tübingen, Germany, in 1964, confirm that all proper healing is from God, disregarding whether it comes through ways following natural laws or not, whether the healing is medical or spiritual, whether we understand how it happened or whether we cannot (yet) explain it. There is no need nor any justification to reject modern medicine as it is a gift of God as well. This also applies however for the use of alternative medicine and special ways of spiritual healing provided their use is according to the values and criteria of Christian faith and critical human discernment. There is nothing which we ought to reject in effective alternative approaches to healing as long as human dignity and freedom are respected in a spirit of love, compassion and acceptance. There is no hierarchy between the different approaches to healing. What we need are round table meetings on regional and national levels leading to dialogue and encounter between people from different approaches to healing, so as to reach a better understanding of the complementary nature of many approaches. Too often, these are not in an honest dialogue with each other.

7. A biblical understanding of holistic healing

The proclamation of the gospel and acts of healing grace were inseparably linked in the ministry of Jesus. According to the biblical understanding health and healing have an essential religious dimension. Healing cannot be reduced to a functional perception in which only one part of the human being (e.g. the physical) is affected. Most prominent in the Bible is a relational understanding of healing as a dynamic process in which a proper and right balance is maintained between different dimensions of relationship. The biblical understanding refers to our relation to ourselves, to our body, as well as to our family, to the larger community in society, as well as to nature as a whole and to the source of all being, God. No dimension (spiritual, physical, social, ecological) should be left out in principle in a holistic understanding of healing. Any proper process of healing has implications for each of these fundamental dimensions of the human being. The spiritual or religious dimension should not be bypassed or dealt with only as an optional, private or merely individual affair. Any understanding of the modern medical system which bypasses, suppresses or ridicules the religious dimension of healing is in danger of absolutising itself at the expense of the wholeness of human existence. Any understanding of spiritual healing which rejects, ignores or avoids the help which can be offered by the achievements of modern medicine is in danger of isolating itself at the expense of the wholeness of human existence.

8. Participants in local or regional healing ministries of the church

It is important to realise that thanks to different gifts of healing, many persons with different trainings can contribute to the overall healing task and ministry of the church. People in medical and caring professions belong to this group as well as lay people in visiting groups, people working in counselling services or people with special gifts in spiritual healing (spiritual healers). Very often the different people active in healing ministries consciously or unconsciously do not know each other or don't recognise each other sufficiently in the local congregations. To increase the sense of ownership and participation in the overall healing ministry, it is advisable that on certain occasions (two to four times a year) the group of all those active in healing ministries be made visible in a special worship occasion to the whole local church.

9. Forms of healing ministries

The following count among the most usual forms of healing ministries in local congregations, hospitals or hospices:

• Intercession, private or public
• laying on of hands
• anointing with oil
• reconciliation and absolution
• healing the family tree
• healing of memories
• self-organised groups of people in need (self-help groups; e.g. Alcoholics Anonymous)
• visiting the sick
• praying groups for people with illnesses

- counselling services
- hospice centres and people accompanying the dying
- prayers for deliverance from evil spirits (exorcism)

It is important that each congregation recognises and encourages the different gifts and talents related to those different forms of healing ministries in its own midst.

10. Accountability and official commissioning for healing ministries

Each ongoing activity in a healing ministry needs a deliberate and public commission if it is to be carried out on behalf of the Christian congregation as a whole and not just as a private affair. Any gift of healing – in the medical, counselling, praying, spiritual or therapeutic field, performed in an explicit Christian term of reference – needs continuous accompaniment, encouragement, evaluation, as well as an accountability structure within the local church. Those active in any of the healing ministries should be made accountable to local church authorities and should receive supervision and personal encouragement in some regular rhythm. In larger churches a key person should be found and appointed to exercise a ministry of oversight and training for a variety of healing ministries exercised in the region.

11. Confidentiality and publicity in healing ministries

Safeguards are needed: the personal sphere of persons seeking healing should be protected and no details from any confidential counselling setting be made public against the will of the persons concerned. Participating in rituals and liturgical celebrations of healing is a matter of trust and requires an atmosphere of protection. Healing services and liturgies must not become demonstrative events or missionary tools utilised by some for the purposes of personal aggrandizement or the goal of a personality show.

12. Miracles, signs and wonders in healing ministries

It is part of the freedom of the work of the Holy Spirit to manifest itself beyond normal understanding during worship services or liturgies focusing on healing transformations and healing processes. But the attention of people participating should not be narrowly focused on so-called "supernatural" events. God's healing energies are at work in manifold ways, in normal ways of healing as well as in ways which cannot yet be explained. Any understanding of healing which fails to recognize the ongoing unchangeable suffering fails to unfold the unconditional love of God to those who have to bear and cope with physical limitations or pain despite intense prayer for healing.

13. Ecumenical cooperation in healing ministries

Gifts and experiences of healing are not the property of just one Christian denomination or confessional tradition. There are immense potentials for learning from each other and enriching each other thanks to different approaches to healing between the different Christian traditions and churches in the world. It would be helpful if an ecumenical advisory board for developing healing ministries be set up locally or regionally to stimulate ecumenical cooperation and mutual learning for churches. Such a body could also start a deliberate common training for healing ministries in regional settings.

14. Spiritual dangers in dealing with healing gifts

God is always the healer, human beings are only channels, instruments and ambassadors of healing and reconciliation. As is the case in the world of therapeutic services there is the danger that persons with healing gifts willingly or unwillingly create in the minds of those seeking healing a sense of dependence from their personality. It should be underlined that healing does not aim at nor require admiration for individual healing gifts. Nor does it depend on a mood of obedience and discipleship towards individual charismatic persons. The healing responsibility of local congregations aims on the contrary at liberating persons - the suffering victims themselves first - to unfold and unleash healing and reconciling energies within themselves so as to become active agents for the healing and reconciling work of God's Spirit in the world.

15. Training, teaching and education in healing ministries

Training and education for healing ministries, equipping the people of God for a holistic understanding and ministry of healing, is an important and indispensable part of the missionary responsibility of the regional church. Training programmes for healing should not only be accessible to people with an academic or professional background in fields of health care and health-related services. The specialisation which is certainly needed in special diaconal institutions should be counterbalanced with an approach recognising spiritual healing gifts also among those persons not professionally working in health-related institutions and positions, but who still can and do contribute substantially to the overall healing ministry of the local church.

Dr Dietrich Werner, Hamburg, Breklum

NOTES

Printed in France by I.M.E.
25110 Baume-les-Dames